CH

D1617573

Calamity Jane

Legends of the Wild West

Sitting Bull

Billy the Kid

Calamity Jane

Buffalo Bill Cody

Crazy Horse

Davy Crockett

Wyatt Earp

Geronimo

Wild Bill Hickok

Jesse James

Nat Love

Annie Oakley

Legends of the Wild West

Calamity Jane

Adam Woog

CHELSEA HOUSE PUBLISHERS

An imprint of Infobase Publishing

For my dad, an honorary resident of the Old West

Calamity Jane

Copyright © 2010 by Infobase Publishing

All rights reserved. No part of this book may be reproduced or utilized in any form or by any means, electronic or mechanical, including photocopying, recording, or by any information storage or retrieval systems, without permission in writing from the publisher. For information, contact:

Chelsea House
An imprint of Infobase Publishing
132 West 31st Street
New York NY 10001

Library of Congress Cataloging-in-Publication Data
Woog, Adam, 1953–
  Calamity Jane / Adam Woog.
    p. cm. — (Legends of the wild West)
  Includes bibliographical references and index.
  ISBN 978-1-60413-595-4 (hardcover)
  1. Calamity Jane, 1852–1903—Juvenile literature. 2. Women pioneers—West (U.S.)—Biography—Juvenile literature. 3. Pioneers—West (U.S.)—Biography—Juvenile literature. 4. West (U.S.)—Biography—Juvenile literature. I. Title. II. Series.
  F594.C2W66 2010
  978'.02092—dc22
  [B]   2010009979

Chelsea House books are available at special discounts when purchased in bulk quantities for businesses, associations, institutions, or sales promotions. Please call our Special Sales Department in New York at (212) 967-8800 or (800) 322-8755.

You can find Chelsea House on the World Wide Web at
http://www.chelseahouse.com

Text design by Kerry Casey
Cover design by Keith Trego
Composition by EJB Publishing Services
Cover printed by Bang Printing, Brainerd, Minn.
Book printed and bound by Bang Printing, Brainerd, Minn.
Date printed: August 2010
Printed in the United States of America

10 9 8 7 6 5 4 3 2 1

This book is printed on acid-free paper.

CONTENTS

THE NOTORIOUS CALAMITY JANE

She was a good woman, only she drank.
>—*Charles Wroe, a cowboy who knew*
>*Calamity Jane in the 1880s*

Some people call her one of the most colorful and freewheeling characters in the Old West. Others say she was a pioneer for women's rights, unafraid to wear trousers and do a man's job in a time when that was scandalous behavior. Some people admire her generosity and selfless work in aid of the ill or destitute. And some believe that she was nothing more than an alcoholic, foul-mouthed, poverty-stricken, good-for-nothing scoundrel. But she was Calamity Jane, and—no matter what anyone says about her otherwise—she was still one of a kind: larger than life, self-reliant, and stubbornly free-spirited.

Many historians feel that of all the legendary figures to emerge from the American frontier, Calamity Jane is one of the least understood. Thanks to such dubious sources as her brief autobiography, *The Life and Adventures of Calamity Jane, by Herself*, her legend has become so encrusted with false stories that it is almost impossible to separate the true from the fanciful.

This is one important reason why she is so misunderstood. So few facts about her are clear. Even the most basic information, such as her exact birth date and the number of her siblings, is uncertain. Strong evidence indicates that she had at least one child of her own, but if so, the identities of their fathers are unclear. Furthermore, at least two other women in the Old West also went by the nickname Calamity Jane, and the three probably crossed paths on occasion, thus confusing the issue even further. Also, there are large gaps in the chronology of her travels and whereabouts.

Even the frontierswoman's real name is uncertain. It was probably Martha Canary, though many variants have appeared: Martha Cannary, Marthy Jane Cannary, Martha Jane Canary Burke, Mattie King, and more. Nonetheless, most people, then and now, simply called her some variation of Calamity Jane.

Meanwhile, adding to the misunderstandings about Calamity Jane, there are all those fanciful stories that she and others told. Jane loved to talk about herself, usually bragging and exaggerating shamelessly. As her fame grew, other hard-living dwellers in the Old West also embroidered her adventures—whether or not they actually knew her. In the decades since, untold numbers of still more outlandish stories and fanciful yarns have been told about her.

An article in the newspaper of one of the many towns the frontierswoman frequented, the Livingston, Montana, *Enterprise*, summed this up in 1887. The anonymous writer, while noting that many of the tales about her were somewhat less than squeaky-clean, commented, "A complete and true biography of Calamity Jane would make a large book, more interesting and blood-curdling than all the fictitious stories that have been written of her, but it would never find its way into a Sunday school library."

AFTER THE ROMANTIC ADVENTURES ARE REMOVED

In some ways, considering her widespread fame as a figure of the Old West, Calamity Jane is as remarkable for what she did *not* do as she

Martha Jane Canary, better known as Calamity Jane, lived a colorful, adventurous life. During her lifetime, Calamity Jane took any job she could, including work as a scout for the military, a cook, a waitress, a dance-hall girl, and a trick shooter for Buffalo Bill's Wild West.

is for what she *did* do. As far as anyone knows, she was not guilty of many of the misdeeds that made other figures in the Old West famous. There is, for instance, no proof that she ever killed anyone. Also, despite her claims, many eyewitnesses say that she was not a good shot or even a particularly good horsewoman. Furthermore, she robbed no banks, chased no criminals, and built no cities or railroads.

In many ways, in fact, she lived a fairly typical and ordinary life for her time and place. Like so many others in that freewheeling environment, Jane moved frequently from town to town, taking on whatever work she could find. As Calamity Jane's most reputable biographer, James D. McLaird, writes in his book *Calamity Jane: The Woman and the Legend*, "Sadly, after romantic adventures are removed, her story is mostly an account of uneventful daily life interrupted by drinking binges."

And yet she packed a tremendous amount into a few short years, living her life with tremendous energy. Furthermore, Jane did pretty much just what she pleased, not caring if people thought she was strange or irresponsible. Often, this was because she did things that women in that time and place simply did not do.

For example, Calamity Jane sometimes wore male clothing. She was as tough as any man, and she could handle a team of horses with skill. She thought nothing of traveling long distances and living in the roughest of circumstances. Jane could also drink even the hardiest drinker under the table. She caroused to excess, sometimes landing in jail for a night or two. She loved to gamble, and she swore foully. She also chewed tobacco and smoked cigars, sometimes at the same time.

On the other hand, Jane sometimes showed that she could act like a typical woman of her time and place. For example, she often found work doing jobs that were usually reserved for women, such as cooking and doing laundry. (She also, almost certainly, was a "scarlet lady" [a term used for women who worked in brothels] off and on, for many years.)

Furthermore, Jane was also well known throughout the West for another typically female characteristic: tenderly nurturing the

Calamity Jane was obsessed with scout and professional gambler Wild Bill Hickok, later claiming that she had married him. Her claim was later proved to be untrue. In fact, they had only known each other for a couple of weeks before Hickok was shot and killed in August 1876.

sick and dying. Writer Margot Mifflin, in her Salon.com article "The Real Calamity Jane," quotes a man who knew her well. He commented that she often was "the last person to hold the head of and administer consolation to the troubled gambler or erstwhile bad man who was about to depart into the new country."

KNOWING WILD BILL

Another aspect of Calamity Jane's fame is that her name is closely intertwined with those of other legendary figures. One of them is George Armstrong Custer, who would become famous after disastrously losing a battle while on a mission to subdue Indians. Another is Buffalo Bill Cody, a flamboyant scout and hunter who became a household name with his enormously popular Wild West shows.

But there is one icon of the Old West with whom Jane will be forever associated more than any other: James Butler Hickok, better known as Wild Bill. Calamity Jane was infatuated and obsessed with this gambler and gunslinger, and she always insisted that she and he were passionately involved with each other. In later years, Jane sometimes even claimed that Hickok was her husband and the father of her child. Jane is even buried next to him in Deadwood, in what is now South Dakota. According to legend, this was her final wish.

However, most serious historians believe that this connection is merely one of the many inflated stories about Calamity Jane. Evidence clearly indicates that the two knew each for only a few weeks, and that Wild Bill never had any desire to be any closer to Jane than as casual acquaintances. Hickok expert Joseph Rosa notes: "[O]f all the women associated in any way with Wild Bill, she had the least to do with him, yet she is always spoken of in the same breath when Hickok's women friends are mentioned."

The many stories told about the frontierswoman's adventures may have cemented her fame, and even today they still make for thrilling reading. Some of these tales may even be true. Despite the distortions and exaggerations, however, and even stripped to nothing but the known facts, Calamity Jane's story is still full of flavor and color. That story began in a farming community in Missouri in the years before the Civil War.

CALAMITY JANE'S EARLY YEARS

The uncertain circumstances of Calamity Jane's birth date and birthplace are just two examples of the fog that shrouds her early history. Sources have variously stated that she was born in 1844, 1847, 1851, 1852, 1856, or 1860 in Princeton, Missouri; Burlington, Iowa; La Salle, Illinois; Salt Lake City, Utah; or Fort Laramie, Wyoming Territory.

Even the exact spelling of Jane's family name is a matter of speculation. Her autobiography states that she was born Martha Jane Cannary on May 1, 1852. It is likely, however, that Calamity could neither read nor write, and variations in spelling were rarely of much concern in the Old West, so this may not be correct.

According to the most thoroughly researched account of her life, James D. McLaird's *Calamity Jane: The Woman and the Legend*, Martha was most likely born in May of 1856 at her family's home near Princeton, in Mercer County, Missouri. Her mother, Charlotte, was about 16 and her father, Robert, about 31 at the time of her birth. McLaird states as evidence that the 1860 census report for Mercer County lists Martha as four years old, the oldest child of Robert and Charlotte Canary. According to this report, there were two other children in the family at the time: three-year-old Cilus and one-year-old Lana.

LIFE IN MERCER COUNTY

Martha was born during a turbulent time for Missouri. In the mid-1850s, the state was a prominent crossroads for America. Its under-populated regions were rapidly being settled by farmers. At the same time, its largest city, St. Louis, was a major starting point for settlers headed to the frontiers of the West and Southwest. Even so, the state was connected only tenuously to the more settled eastern United States, and Missourians were largely on their own to create lives for themselves.

As for politics, Missouri was a slaveholding state then. It is not clear where the Canary family's sympathies lay in this conflict; as far as is known, however, the family did not own slaves. In any case, they would not have been able to escape the issue of slavery entirely. In a few years, Missouri would become a central part of the battle to end this practice. Slavery had passionate and often violent support-ers on both sides of the issue—a situation that would lead, in a few years, to the Civil War.

Mercer County, in the north central part of the state on the Iowa border, had been organized by settlers only about a decade before Martha was born. In fact, the region probably had no white settlers until the 1830s. Previously, it had been important hunting grounds for tribes of Fox, Sioux, and Potawatomi Indians.

The Canarys probably moved there shortly before Martha was born. They came from Ohio, where both Robert and Charlotte had grown up. The family moved to an area that was still sparsely populated, and still a region dominated by farmers raising live-stock and growing such crops as corn, oats, wheat, tobacco, and potatoes. They lived on land that Robert bought from his father, who continued to live with them. The 1860 census report for Mer-cer County noted that their farm was about 7 miles (11 km) north-east of Princeton in the hamlet of Ravanna.

Like many people in sparsely populated regions of the coun-try, the Canarys pursued a variety of occupations to make ends meet. As far as is known, Robert was primarily a farmer and a some-time gambler. According to some sources, Charlotte had once been

Many people looking for a better life took advantage of the offer from Congress to settle land in the West. People like the Canarys packed all of their possessions, joined wagon trains, and faced unknown dangers to journey to regions such as Montana Territory. This painting depicts emigrants crossing the Rocky Mountains while being watched by Native Americans.

"a fallen woman," (a common phrase in that era for a woman who has sexual relations outside of marriage) although this is not certain. She was apparently a rather daring and unorthodox woman for her time, scandalizing the neighbors by smoking cigars and otherwise carrying on. Her daughter Marthy, as she was known, may have inherited her notorious wild streak naturally from her mother.

ON THE TRAIL TO MONTANA TERRITORY

The Canary family did not stay long in Missouri. This was typical of a major characteristic of the Old West: its fluid and constant change.

As the frontier pushed west across America, huge waves of new settlers arrived there, often continuing to move from region to region in search of better work and lives.

The Canarys were no exception, and in 1862 or 1863 the family left Missouri. The family settled briefly in Iowa, to the north. However, probably in 1864 (not 1865 as Calamity Jane states in her autobiography), they were on the move again. The Canarys left Iowa abruptly, and some historians have speculated they may have fled because of debts that could not be paid.

Their destination this time was Virginia City, in the southwest corner of what was then Montana Territory. (Montana did not become a state until 1889.) They traveled as part of a wagon train. These caravans of horse-drawn wagons were a common means of transportation in the West; they allowed travelers to band together for safety and company when crossing the dangerous frontier.

The Canarys' journey was an arduous trek across rugged terrain; it took five months just to travel from Iowa to Montana. Martha, who was about nine at the time, wrote later in her autobiography:

> Many times in crossing the mountains the conditions of the trail were so bad that we frequently had to lower the wagons over ledges by hand with ropes for they were so rough and rugged that horses were of no use. We also had many exciting times fording streams for many of the streams in our way were noted for quicksands and boggy places, where, unless we were very careful, we would have lost horses and all.

LOOKING FOR GOLD IN VIRGINIA CITY

It is likely that Robert Canary moved his family west in search of gold—or at least in search of any work that could be found around gold-mining camps. Huge stores of the precious metal had been found in the isolated mountain region of Alder Gulch in 1863, and almost overnight the tiny settlements around it, including

Virginia City, became bustling boomtowns. Eager prospectors flocked there hoping to try their luck, and many others came to supply them with such services as liveries, saloons, hotels, brothels, and general stores.

Traveling Overland to Virginia City

Calamity Jane described her early life in her autobiography, *Life and Adventures of Calamity Jane, by Herself.* Many of her stories were so embellished that it is hard to know what is fact and what is fiction. Her associations with famous people were almost always claimed once those people were gone and buried, and thus not able to contradict her story. Here is a passage from her book:

As a child I always had a fondness for adventure and out-door exercise and especial fondness for horses which I began to ride at an early age and continued to do so until I became an expert rider being able to ride the most vicious and stubborn of horses, in fact the greater portion of my life in early times was spent in this manner....

While on the way [to Montana] the greater portion of my time was spent in hunting along with the men and hunters of the party, in fact I was at all times with the men when there was excitement and adventures to be had. By the time we reached Virginia City I was considered a remarkable good shot and a fearless rider for a girl of my age....

Then we had many dangers to encounter in the way of streams swelling on account of heavy rains. On occasions of that kind the men would usually select the best places to cross the streams, myself on more than one occasion have mounted my pony and swam across the stream several times merely to amuse myself and have had many narrow escapes from having both myself and pony washed away to certain death, but as the pioneers of those days had plenty of courage we overcame all obstacles and reached Virginia City in safety.

Many miners came to Virginia City, Montana, to look for gold in Alder Gulch. Although Alder Gulch yielded an estimated $30 million in gold between 1863 and 1866, most miners barely made a living. In 1864, the year the Canarys arrived in Virginia City, the town was the largest in the inland Northwest. Today, only 132 people are residents of Virginia City.

Virginia City was the first capital of Montana Territory and the home of its first newspaper (the *Montana Post*) as well as its first public school. Sarah Raymond was one of the many young women, like Martha, who had recently arrived there by wagon train with her family. In a memoir she wrote, Sarah recalled that the rough-and-ready town was the shabbiest place she had ever seen.

However, Sarah also noted that it was one of the busiest. She described the citizens of Virginia City as they scrambled to create a town where there had once been only wilderness. Quoted in McLaird's *Calamity Jane*, she recalls, "It seemed that not one of that great multitude stopped for one instant shoveling and wheeling dirt, passing and repassing each other without a hitch. It made me tired to look at them."

Life was not easy in such a place, and this seems to have been especially true for Martha and her family. Reprinted in Roberta Beed Sollid's book *Calamity Jane*, the *Montana Post* reported in December 1864 that Martha and two of her siblings were seen asking for handouts. (Another child had clearly arrived in the family. According to different sources, there were four to six Canary siblings; all sources agree, however, that Martha was the eldest.) The paper wrote:

> Three little girls, who state their name to be Canary, appeared on the door of Mr. Fergus, on Idaho Street, soliciting charity. The ages of the two elder ones were about ten and twelve, respectively. The eldest girl carried in her arms her infant sister, a baby of about twelve months of age. Canary, the father, it seems, is a gambler [and the] mother is a woman of the lowest grade.

Fergus was the county commissioner, so he was in charge of caring for the poor. Noting that the three girls were hungry and poorly dressed for the cold of a Montanan December, Fergus and his wife supplied them with adequate food and warm clothes.

This relief was temporary, however, and the Canary family continued to experience misfortune. In 1866, Martha's mother died, the victim of a respiratory disease known as washerwoman's pneumonia. Charlotte had been supplementing the family's income by taking in washing, and her illness was a common one among women like her who did laundry on the frontier. The combination of wet, cold conditions and infectious diseases carried in clothing and bedding was often deadly.

MARTHA STRIKES OUT ON HER OWN

After his wife passed away, Martha's father moved the family to Salt Lake City, Utah. Some historians speculate that he may have meant to continue east and return to Missouri eventually. In any case, he stayed in Salt Lake City, acquired 40 acres (16 hectares) of land, and began to farm it. His new beginning was short-lived, however; about a year after the move, Robert also died.

The Canary children, now orphans, were left to their own devices. An adoptive family likely took the siblings in for a period, but soon they were on their own. Still in her early teens, Martha was now the head of a family that was far from relatives, friends, and familiar environments.

Soon after her father's death, Martha struck out for new territory on her own. It is not clear why she chose to leave her brothers and sisters, or what the other children did at this point. However, it is a reasonable assumption that foster families in the Salt Lake City region took them in, at least temporarily.

This time Martha journeyed to a region even less settled than Utah: Wyoming Territory. In the spring of 1868, she settled in the southwest Wyoming town of Piedmont. Seven thousand feet (2,133.6 meters) up in the region's mountains, Piedmont was a rough little settlement that owed its existence to the building of wooden ties for railroads. Specifically, it was a company town for the Union Pacific railway system, which was then about a year away from becoming the nation's first transcontinental railway.

In this regard, Piedmont was typical of the towns that had sprung up along the railway line as it progressed across the country. Thanks to these towns, the territory was becoming rapidly settled. In November 1868, the *Frontier Index* newspaper noted that within the past year the population of Wyoming had grown from less than 1,000 to more than 35,000.

Quoted in McLaird's *Calamity Jane: The Woman and the Legend*, the newspaper stated that Piedmont's population was made up of "adventurous and energetic men," such as lumbermen, ranchers, miners, merchants, construction workers, a few professionals such as doctors and lawyers, as well as a number of unsavory and shady types: "[G]amblers in profusion, and a full complement of other characters who do not reflect much credit on any place they infest."

ENTERTAINING AT THE THREE-MILE HOG RANCH AND OTHER JOBS

Martha seemed to fit in well to this freewheeling atmosphere. Once settled in the Piedmont area, she took on whatever jobs she could find. She worked as a dishwasher, cook, laundress, waitress, dance hall girl, nurse, and ox team driver. According to several sources, she also found occasional employment as a scarlet lady at the Three-Mile Hog Ranch, a "social center" that entertained the military men stationed at the U.S. Army's nearby Fort Laramie.

Calamity did not stay long—a fact that reflected her lifelong inability to stay in one place for any length of time. Soon, she was working her way east, probably paying her way as a menial laborer, laundress, and possibly, again, as a scarlet lady. She spent time in several Wyoming towns, including Rawlins and Laramie, before stopping for a time in Cheyenne, in the far southeast corner of the state.

Like Piedmont, Cheyenne had been born when it was the end of the line for the westbound construction of the Union Pacific. Unlike some of the other towns along the route, however, it had managed to thrive even after the railroad progressed further west. By the early 1870s, when Martha arrived there, it had become the capital of Wyoming Territory. (Wyoming became a state in 1890.)

In terms of economics, meanwhile, Cheyenne had shifted from being dominated by the railroad to being a cattle town. This meant that it was a major terminal point for the huge cattle herds that were then being driven north from Texas. These animals would be sold in Cheyenne and shipped by rail to markets in eastern states. Adding to the life of the town, meanwhile, was the presence of U.S. Army troops at nearby Camp Carlin, later called Fort Russell (and now Warren Air Force Base). Like the other army forts in the West, Carlin was primarily designed to quell American Indian uprisings and to protect white settlers arriving from the East.

Despite its status as the territorial capital, the town at the time was hardly a civilized place in the usual sense of the word. For one thing, it was growing so fast that, like other boomtowns, living space was scarce—and what was available was rudimentary. In an 1887 newspaper interview, reprinted in McLaird's biography on Calamity Jane, Martha recalled, "When I first came to Cheyenne there was not a respectable shelter in the place, and the proprietor of a tent was a lucky person indeed."

As was true for the Old West in general, it was a particularly rough environment for women. On the other hand, Wyoming was unusually enlightened in some ways, at least in terms of women's rights. Notably, women in the territory could vote and even hold office, a right not granted nationally until 1920. Nonetheless, the normal opportunities for females in a cattle town like Cheyenne were limited—and Martha was never interested in confining herself to anything like a normal life, as the following years proved.

RIDING
WITH THE ARMY

While living in the Cheyenne area, Martha was able to find work that suited her rough-and-ready personality and supported her reluctance to be hampered by her gender—that is, if her autobiography is to be believed. According to that document, she was hired as a scout for the U.S. Army.

As such, she claimed, she guided regiments of soldiers across regions of what would become Arizona, North and South Dakota, Wyoming, and Montana as part of the military's ongoing efforts to subdue the region's American Indians. She later wrote in her autobiography:

> Was in Arizona up to the winter of 1871 and during that time I had a great many adventures with the Indians, for as a scout I had a great many dangerous missions to perform and while I was in many close places always succeeded in getting away safely for by this time I was considered the most reckless and daring rider and one of the best shots in the western country.

As is true with other parts of her autobiography, however, many of her contemporaries, as well as future historians, have questioned this claim. They have expressed doubt that she was a scout in any capacity, much less one capable of leading large numbers of soldiers through unknown terrain.

For one thing, Martha was still a teenager—and a teenage girl, at that—in an environment that did not easily accept women in a job like scouting. For another, she was still relatively unfamiliar with that region. Therefore, it would have been very unusual for the army to have hired her for such skilled work. Furthermore, if she had indeed worked as a scout, it would have been extraordinary news, and it surely would have been noted in local newspapers. In any case, no mention of Martha scouting has been found in any of the newspapers from that era, or in official military records.

Even if it cannot be proved that Martha was indeed an army scout as she claimed, there is some evidence that the military informally hired her at one point as a wagon driver. Buffalo Bill Cody later told reporters that he rode with Martha on at least one expedition during this period.

Cody recalled her as a good hunter and perfectly at home in rough country. However, he also said that she was never more than what was generally called a camp follower. This term generally referred to civilians who tagged along with (and were sometimes hired by) military regiments on the move. The term also was sometimes used as a euphemism for a scarlet lady.

As noted in McLaird's biography, Cody recalled her as being generally amiable and well liked. He stated: "[S]he would join different military expeditions as a kind of hanger on, and generally joined them so far away from the settlements that it would be cruel for a commanding officer to send her away from the command or put her under arrest. Everyone knew and liked her, and dubbed her 'mascot'; and were generally glad to have her along with the company."

No matter what her real capacity was with the U.S. Army, the young woman had clearly found an environment in which she felt comfortable. She liked action, liveliness, and adventure, and she was not afraid of hard work. In *Calamity Jane: The Woman and the Legend*, McLaird points this out when he comments, "Although Martha's role with the military . . . has been greatly exaggerated, her

During her time working with the army, Calamity Jane served as a scout with Buffalo Bill Cody. Later, Calamity Jane would work for Cody as a sharpshooter in his Wild West show. Pictured is Calamity Jane with Buffalo Bill Cody.

[life] did require physical endurance and placed her in considerable personal danger.... Obviously, she thrived on danger."

BECOMING CALAMITY JANE

At some point during this period, Martha Canary acquired her famous nickname, although its origins are obscure. For one thing, there is no documented proof that her middle name was actually Jane, as she asserted after she became famous. Nor is it clear at what point she began to be known as Jane more often than she was called Martha.

As for the first part of her nickname, there are many versions of how it came about. One story relates that she was so named because she would warn men that to offend her was to "court calamity." Other stories relate that she was Calamity because of her chaotic past as an orphan, because she was always getting in trouble, or because she shouted "What a calamity" when she lost at poker.

Jane herself always maintained that an army captain named Egan was the first person to call her Calamity Jane. According to this story, it came about when she was attached to the captain's unit at Little Goose Creek, Wyoming, near the Montana border and what is now the town of Sheridan.

At one point on the journey, she related, a group of American Indian warriors ambushed some soldiers being led by Captain Egan. Egan was shot during the fight and Jane saw him nearly fall off his horse. She galloped to his side, caught the wounded officer just before he fell to the ground, hauled him onto her horse behind her, and rode safely back to the fort. According to her autobiography, Egan "laughingly said, 'I name you Calamity Jane, the heroine of the plains.' I have borne that name up to the present time."

This version of events makes for a good story, but—like so many of Jane's statements—it is probably not true. For one thing, Egan's wife always denied the tale; for another, so did several officers who knew the captain. Nonetheless, the story quickly took hold in the popular imagination. Historian Roberta Sollid notes that it perfectly fit the public image that Jane wanted to project. In *Calamity Jane*, Sollid remarks: "Egan was a colorful personality and the kind of man with whom Calamity would have liked to be permanently linked."

An indication that the young woman was becoming well known as Calamity Jane, or simply Calamity, is the first known reference to that nickname in a newspaper. In June 1875, the *Chicago Tribune* quoted an unknown Western scout remarking that it would be a great calamity if his friend Jane were to be captured by Indians.

THE BATTLE OF THE LITTLE BIG HORN

As the 1870s progressed, Calamity Jane accompanied a number of notable military expeditions. In later years, she claimed that one of the era's most famous U.S. generals, George Armstrong Custer, hired her as a scout on an expedition from Fort Russell into Arizona Territory. Numerous historians have disputed this claim, pointing out that Custer was not at Fort Russell and never participated in an Arizona campaign.

As many people know, Custer earned his place in history books primarily for one disastrous confrontation: a battle at the Little Big Horn River in the Black Hills of Dakota Territory. In May 1876, leading a campaign against the American Indians, Custer made a fatal mistake: He moved his troops in to attack a huge gathering of American Indians from the Lakota, Northern Cheyenne, and Arapaho tribes. These groups had been called together by the legendary Lakota leader Sitting Bull to discuss how to handle the white settlers encroaching on their land. Custer was killed in the ensuing conflict, which ended as a decisive victory for the American Indians.

Some accounts of Calamity Jane's life, including her autobiography, state that she believed she could have warned Custer to avoid the massacre. In an interview cited in McLaird's biography, Jane told a reporter in Glendive, Montana: "I was with Custer for several months and in different engagements, but if I had been with him in his last battle, I would probably be [dead] with him now. On the other hand, had Custer paid attention to warnings and a message I sent him he and his brave band might be now in the land that I am in."

CARRYING "LIQUID AMMUNITION" IN HER SADDLEBAGS

Like so many of Calamity Jane's statements, this intimation that she knew Custer must be taken skeptically. Only one instance has been definitively shown in which she even met the general, much less worked for him or was a trusted adviser. It appears, however, that she was associated with another general of the time, George Crook, who did lead expeditions into Arizona, Wyoming, and the Dakota territories. One of these, which Jane probably accompanied, was a campaign to quell an uprising by the Muscle Shell Indians (an event sometimes called the Nursey Pursey uprising) in central Wyoming Territory.

Another incident when Calamity Jane encountered Crook's troops came in the late summer of 1876. The military man and his soldiers were forced to retreat following major battles with Lakota and Cheyenne Indians. The

In 1875, Calamity Jane posed as a man and joined General George Crook's Black Hills force against the Sioux Indians. Crook (*above*) was believed to be the best American Indian fighter the army has ever produced. Later one of Crook's officers found out Calamity Jane was a woman and had her expelled.

army troops were in rough shape, having suffered serious casualties and finding precious little to eat. Toward the end of their grueling journey, the soldiers were forced to slaughter some of their own horses for meat.

Crook and his soldiers finally connected with a rescue party in what is now Lawrence County, South Dakota. The rescuers were able to find the desperate troops and deliver much-needed supplies.

Jane was one member of this party. Valentine T. McGillycuddy, a doctor who was traveling with Crook's group, wrote in his journal (excerpted in Candy Moulton's article in *True West* magazine, "Following Calamity Jane") about "our old friend Calamity," who had changed considerably since McGillycuddy had last seen her. The doctor wrote that she had "blossomed out as a fully equipped border scout, beaded buckskin trousers, blue shirt, broad brimmed hat, Winchester rifle, mounted on a bucking broncho[sic], with a supply of fluid ammunition [liquor] in the saddle bags."

During the mid-1870s, Jane also traveled with at least one regiment of soldiers into the Black Hills of Dakota Territory. This was an operation to protect the Newton-Jenney party, a geological expedition that had set out to determine the value of mineral deposits in the region—especially gold. She later stated that the group's mission was simply to protect miners and settlers there from hostile bands of Lakota Sioux Indians.

Jane's adventures in the Black Hills during the 1870s were just the beginning of a lifelong connection she would have with the region. The Black Hills—an isolated and heavily forested mountain range rising dramatically from the expanses of Great Plains—clearly held a particular fascination for the outdoorswoman.

Calamity Jane liked to boast that she was the first white woman to venture into the Black Hills. Evidence indicates that she was not the first, but she was certainly one of the first Caucasian women to explore this remote country. Quoted in McLaird's biography, she told a reporter in 1896 with characteristic exaggeration, "Wa'n't nothin' here but a few miners, an' they wouldn't have been here if me

"My! How She Did Swear at Me"

An army surgeon who doubled as a correspondent for the *Chicago Tribune* gave the world one of the earliest detailed accounts of Calamity Jane. She was then a teamster. Quoted in McLaird's biography, the surgeon wrote on June 19, 1875: "Calam is dressed in a suit of soldier's blue, and straddles a mule equal to any professional blacksnake swinger in the army. . . .Calamity also jumps upon a trooper's horse and rides along in the ranks, and gives an officer a military [salute] with as much style as the First corporal in a crack company."

During this period in her life, early in her career on the frontier, Calamity was already demonstrating that she could withstand a lot—but also that, when she was mad, she did not keep her feelings to herself. On one occasion, a freight carrier named Sam Young was in charge of a horse-drawn wagon in which Jane was riding. It overturned in a creek, and (as also quoted in McLaird's book) Young commented, "Calamity, being under the wagon sheet, was compelled to crawl out of the hind end, and in doing so, fell in the water up to her neck. My! How she did swear at me; and she always seemed to have the idea that I did it purposely, but such was not the case."

an' the soldiers hadn't come and took 'em [the Hills] away from the Injuns. Yes, I was a regular man in them days. I knew every creek an' holler from the Missouri to the Pacific."

WEARING PANTS, DRINKING HEAVILY, AND SLEEPING COLD

Calamity Jane probably meant her remark about being "a regular man" simply to mean that she could do any job a man could do. There is another aspect to this remark, however. At some point during this period, Jane had started wearing men's clothing on a regular basis—something that today is certainly not unusual, but which was remarkable in that time and place.

Sometimes, she wore an outfit of buckskin clothing, like the one McGillycuddy noted. She was also sometimes seen wearing an army uniform. This may have been done to avoid being detected as a woman, since some commanding officers would have banished her if they knew she was a woman, and would certainly not have considered her for dangerous, difficult, or dirty work.

Jane did not dress in men's clothes all the time, however. She often wore conventional dresses, especially later in her life. The main reason she often opted for trousers and shirts was simply that such durable clothing was infinitely more comfortable and practical in her rugged world.

During this time, one wagon-train captain later recalled that he saw Calamity Jane, then about 20, driving a mule team en route to the Black Hills from Cheyenne. He noted that she was wearing a buckskin suit. The captain also commented that Jane was already fond of alcohol. He stated, in a passage noted in McLaird's biography, "The first place that attracted her attention was a saloon, where she was soon made blind as a bat from looking through the bottom of a glass."

During this period, Jane also demonstrated that she was an unusually hardy individual. She rarely minded "sleeping cold," or out in the open with little in the way of bedding. She also liked to boast that she was rarely ill. One of the few reported incidents of illness (until late in her life) came in 1875, when she was accompanying an expedition led by General Crook on the Big Horn River.

In order to carry messages, Martha said in her autobiography, she forded the Platte River and traveled some 90 miles (145 km) at top speed while wet and cold. After completing her mission, she fell ill and needed several weeks to recuperate at Fort Fetterman in Dakota Territory. However, historians have questioned this story. They note that all of the couriers used in that campaign were named in official documents, and that Jane's name was not among them.

Calamity Jane was known for her unconventional ways and was respected by the men on the frontier. As a young girl, she enjoyed hunting, riding horses, and fishing with her father and brothers. Later, she gained a notable reputation as a sharpshooter, worked as an army scout, chewed tobacco, drank alcohol, and wore men's clothes.

JANE BEHAVING BADLY

In between forays with the military, Calamity Jane apparently also worked in businesses called "road ranches" that sprang up between Fort Russell and Fort Laramie. Road ranches were crude stopover points for soldiers and travelers along trails in the Old West. They offered a night's lodging and food, and typically the company of scarlet ladies as well.

One of the establishments where Jane found work was Coffee's Ranch. Quoted in McLaird's *Calamity Jane*, a U.S. army sergeant, John Q. Ward, recalled that it was a well-known and popular locale:

> Coffee's Ranch was known to every soldier, mule skinner, bull whacker, cowpuncher, packer, gambler and bad man for hundreds of miles up and down the Platte River, and it was at this place Calamity acted as an entertainer—dancing, drinking much bad whisky and in various ways relieving her victims of their coin, which she spent with a free and willing hand.

Clearly, Jane was on her way to becoming a notorious figure. More and more often, her bad behavior was mentioned in the region's newspapers, which noted that she regularly got into trouble. In 1876, for instance, she was arrested in Cheyenne. After a drinking spree, she had tried to steal several items from a store, including skirts worth $7.00, stockings worth $0.50, a petticoat worth $2.50, and a $2.00 hat.

The thief spent some three weeks in jail awaiting trial. She had no suitable clothes for a court appearance—that was why she had been stealing skirts, after all—so the sheriff's wife lent her a dress. When the court found Calamity Jane not guilty, she triumphantly walked through the streets of Cheyenne in the borrowed dress. According to people who were there, this mortified the sheriff's wife, for it implied wrongly that she and the notorious Calamity Jane were friends.

When she was done with her victory march, Jane promptly got drunk again. According to legend, at the end of this alcoholic spree she rented a horse and buggy, intending to go the short distance to Fort Russell, Wyoming. Jane was so drunk, however, that she overshot her destination by 50 miles (80.5 kilometers), stopped at a road ranch overnight to drink more, and eventually ended up at Fort Laramie, far away from her original destination. A peace officer found her but did not arrest her for stealing the buggy and horse, instead simply returning them to the livery stable in Cheyenne and letting Calamity go her way.

True to her nature, Calamity did not stay in the Fort Laramie region long. In the summer of 1876, she reached a decisive and fateful turning point in her life. She headed to a thriving mining town called Deadwood.

4

ADVENTURES IN DEADWOOD

The beginnings of Calamity Jane's journey to Deadwood began in 1874. That year, an expedition of soldiers led by General Custer left its base at Fort Lincoln, in Dakota Territory. This assembly included some 1,000 men, 110 wagons, cannons, and hundreds of horses, mules, and cattle—plus newspaper reporters and a photographer to publicize the event. The two-month expedition's official mission was to scout potential sites for a new fort. Unofficially, Custer was also charged with confirming or denying the rumored presence of gold in the Black Hills.

Custer succeeded. Near the western border of what is now South Dakota, he found a large deposit of the precious metal. The general sent a message back to Fort Lincoln announcing his find. Quoted in an anonymous article, "The Custer Expedition," in the July/August 1996 issue of *Deadwood* magazine, the general wrote: "I have on my table forty or fifty small particles of pure gold . . . most of it obtained today from one panful of earth."

Not surprisingly, word of Custer's valuable find quickly spread. By the time the general returned to Fort Lincoln, the Dakota Territory was electric with excitement. Bismarck, Cheyenne, Yankton, and Virginia City were just four of the towns

Despite the long history of the Lakota in the Black Hills of South Dakota, the U.S. government took control of the region after General George Custer discovered gold there. Thousands of miners, some of whom are depicted above, settled in the Black Hills to search for riches. In 1875, Calamity Jane traveled to the region with the Newton-Jenney party.

vying to be starting points for anyone hoping to trek to the goldfields.

Their newspapers did as much as possible to stir up public interest in the potential for riches. In his biography of Calamity Jane, McLaird notes two typical headlines: the Yankton paper trumpeted "Dakota's Mines to Eclipse the World," while Bismarck's paper echoed the sentiment "Gold Enough to Pay the National Debt."

Custer's full report, delivered after his return, added to the gold fever. It stated that the precious metal could be found lying around on open ground and in every stream. He also noted that there was more to the Black Hills that would appeal to anyone hoping to settle there. Quoted in *A History of the Dakota or Sioux Indians* by Doane Robinson, Custer wrote:

> The country which we have passed since leaving the Belle Fourche River has been generally open and very fertile. The main portion of that passed over since entering the unexplored portions of the Black Hills consists of beautiful parks and valleys, through which flow streams of clear, cold water, perfectly free from alkali, which bounding these parks, or valleys, is invariably found unlimited supplies of timber, much of it being capable of being made into good lumber.
>
> In no portion of the United States, not excepting the famous bluegrass region of Kentucky, have I ever seen grazing superior to that found growing wild in this hitherto unknown region. I know of no portion of our country where nature has done so much to prepare homes for husbandmen and left so little for the latter to do as here. The open and timber spaces are so divided that a partly prepared farm of almost any dimensions can be found here.... Cattle could winter in these valleys without other food or shelter than that to be obtained from running at large.

IGNORING THE TREATY

There was a problem, however. The gold-rich land was officially off-limits to whites, except those on official government business. This was because it was part of the Sioux Reservation, a tract of land that had been deeded forever to that tribe in 1868.

Some authorities were willing to conveniently overlook the treaty that established this law, including at least one federal official: U.S. Secretary of the Interior Columbus Delano. In a letter quoted in the *Deadwood* magazine article, he wrote:

> I am inclined to think that the occupation of this region of the country is not necessary to the happiness and

prosperity of the Indians, and as it is supposed to be rich in minerals and lumber it is deemed important to have it freed as early as possible from Indian occupancy.

I shall, therefore, not oppose any policy which looks first to a careful examination of the subject. . . . If such an examination leads to the conclusion that the country is not necessary or useful to Indians, I should then deem it advisable...to extinguish the claim of the Indians and open the territory to the occupation of the whites.

Despite Delano's opinion, the government established a policy preventing miners from coming into the region. Several military leaders, including General Custer, tried to do just that. Their efforts were not successful.

The quantity of gold found in the region was not large compared to others in the 1800s, notably the vast goldfields in California and in the Yukon Territory of Canada. Nonetheless, Dakota Territory's gold was plentiful enough to lure thousands of would-be prospectors with the promise of sudden wealth. At the same time that the rush of fortune seekers began, entrepreneurs set out to serve the prospectors' needs by establishing stores, livery stables, saloons, restaurants, brothels, and more.

Deadwood was only one of several boomtowns that were born as a result of this dash toward promised riches. (The town's name came from a nearby expanse of burned-out forest.) Mary Franz, in her article "The Real Men of Deadwood" from the August 2006 issue of *Wild West* magazine, comments, "Deadwood grew from the promise of wealth."

KNEE-DEEP IN MUD, RATS, AND GARBAGE

Like every other boomtown, Deadwood was created in a makeshift, haphazard hurry. In creating businesses, homes, and other structures, everyone was on his (or, less frequently, her) own. At first, as an estimated 10,000 to 20,000 prospectors passed

The arrival of thousands of gold miners in the Blacks Hills gave rise to boomtowns like Deadwood. These settlements gained a wild reputation for lawlessness during the Black Hills gold rush. In 1876, Calamity Jane traveled with a group that included Wild Bill Hickok and settled in Deadwood, South Dakota.

through the new settlement, it became, Franz notes in her *Wild West* article, "little more than a rough-and-tumble mining camp, where men, livestock and the elements coexisted, in a sprawl of ramshackle buildings and tents, knee-deep in mud, rats and garbage."

In its early days, the political and social organization of Deadwood was as disorganized as its physical layout. Since it was illegally on Indian land, the U.S. government had no official authority there. As a result, for some time the town had no government, written laws, organized peacekeeping, or town planning.

By the end of 1876, however, as the settlement continued to grow, significant changes came to Deadwood. The town's leaders created a rough form of government, including a mayor, a health department, and a court. This was the result of a combination of the need for increased order, a reaction to a fire that devastated many of the town's wooden buildings, and the eventual arrival of a railroad connection. At its peak, Deadwood had some 3,000 full-time residents, 200 businesses, and a number of stone and brick buildings in addition to its wooden structures and tents.

Despite the trappings of an established settlement, however, Deadwood was always a wide-open place where virtually anything could happen—and often did. The saloons and brothels on nearly every street were always crowded, and violence was so common that people claimed Deadwood experienced a murder a day. Furthermore, there was powerful tension between white settlers and the town's community of Chinese immigrants. The continuing presence of American Indians in the region added an extra element of racial unpredictability to the mix as well.

CALAMITY JANE, CHARLIE, AND WILD BILL

Calamity Jane became part of this raw environment in the summer of 1876. She arrived there with a train of 30 wagons that was coming from Colorado with supplies and people to bolster business in Deadwood, including several gamblers and about 180 scarlet ladies. Jane probably joined this group at a spot called Government Farm, 15 miles (24 km) north of Fort Laramie.

Calamity may have willingly joined up with this party; however, according to one source she had little choice. This story has it that the wagon-train leaders took her along with them at the request of a peace officer in Government Farm. After being refused a position with a military expedition, Jane had gotten drunk there, and she became so belligerent that the officer put her in the outpost's guardhouse. He asked the leaders of the passing train to take

Calamity Jane with them, and clothes were donated so that she would have enough for the journey.

The wagon train had three leaders. One of them was a frontiersman known as Charles "Colorado Charlie" Utter. Born in New York State, he had been at various times a prospector, trapper, and guide in the region that gave him his nickname. Utter would go on to become a prominent citizen in Deadwood. Accompanying him was his brother, Steve, and the third partner in the venture: James Butler Hickok, better known as "Wild Bill."

Wild Bill had originally been nicknamed "Duck Bill" for his long nose, a name he understandably changed. Born in Illinois, Hickok had moved to Kansas as a teenager, fought for the Union army during the Civil War, and wandered throughout the West as a law officer, gambler, gunslinger, and guide. He had recently gotten married in Cheyenne in the spring of 1876, wedded to a widowed former circus performer, Agnes Thatcher Lake. The minister who performed the ceremony was apparently not optimistic about the marriage. In his article "Agnes Thatcher Lake: Equestrian Rider, Circus Performer, and Wild Bill's Wife," Phil Roberts, a professor of history at the University of Wyoming, quotes a notation the clergyman made in the records of the First Methodist Church of Cheyenne: "Don't think he meant it."

The minister was right; no matter what Wild Bill's intentions may have been, the marriage was not destined to last. The newlyweds traveled to her hometown of Cincinnati, where she remained while Bill returned to Cheyenne to resume his activities in the West. Partially because failing eyesight was affecting his shooting ability, Wild Bill decided to try his luck prospecting in the gold mines of Deadwood. Already friends with Charlie, Hickok joined the Utter party as a partner with the brothers. He was not to live much longer, however.

CALAMITY JANE HAS ARRIVED

Jane immediately became friends with Charlie Utter—and she became powerfully infatuated with Wild Bill, an emotion she would sustain for the rest of her life. This obsession, however, apparently went only in one direction.

All of the serious research that has been done on the subject, including the collecting of eyewitness testimony, indicates that Hickok was barely even interested in being friends with her. It is also apparent that they did not know each other for long. Joseph C. Rosa, in *Wild Bill Hickok: The Man and the Myth*, comments, "Contemporary reports and the recollections of those who knew both parties very well indicate that they only met weeks before Hickok's death."

No matter how her relationship with Wild Bill was playing out, it is clear that Jane did join the wagon train at Government Farm. After that, it took the group another two weeks to reach the Black Hills. This was a strenuous trip through particularly rough country, and the party encountered a number of obstacles, including stinging insects, drenching rain, deep gulches, and mud so thick that every hundred yards or so it had to be pried off the wheels of the wagons with a crowbar.

Jane, who was now about 25, proved herself useful on the journey. She was already skilled at driving a team of mules and performing other rough jobs as well as any man. The unorthodox woman's reputation for bold behavior evidently preceded her arrival in Deadwood. David Lavery, in his book *Reading Deadwood: A Western to Swear By*, notes that when the wagon train reached the town its local newspaper, the *Black Hills Pioneer,* reported: "Calamity Jane has arrived."

As she always had, once she had settled in town Jane found work wherever she could. For at least some of her time in Deadwood, she worked as a dance hall girl. As the name implies, this was a woman who worked in dance halls (which were often nothing fancier than large tents). The standard practice for dance hall girls was to charge their partners no money for dancing; instead, they would convince the men to buy drinks, splitting the profits with the house. Dance hall girls were not necessarily also scarlet ladies, although that was often the case.

It appears that Calamity Jane worked most frequently at two places: Al Swearingen's Gem Saloon and its rival, the Bella Union.

Both places featured dancing, music, gambling, and prostitution. Evidence indicates that Jane also helped Swearingen recruit new girls for his operation, traveling to nearby towns to find them.

As might be expected, when she was not working Calamity Jane spent most of her time as a customer in Deadwood's saloons. In addition to steadily drinking, she liked to play faro, a popular card game at the time. Calamity's love of a good time—and her fearless willingness to jump into any fracas—led to some scandalous behavior and the occasional stay in a jail.

One report from this time states that Jane also tried her hand at being a brothel madam, running her own "sporting house" for a while to compete with another entrepreneur, Kitty Austin. According to this story, Jane was known to ride up and down the street on a horse, howling and shooting at windows in her rival Kitty's operation.

Legend also has it that one night Jane and a friend, a gunslinger known as Arkansas Tom, attended a show given by a traveling troupe of actors at Deadwood's East Lynne Opera House. Jane disliked the end of the play, however, and to register her displeasure she spat a stream of tobacco juice at the stage, hitting the star in the eye. Then Tom shot out the lamps and the crowd cheered.

Another well-known story about Calamity Jane's time in Deadwood was told to support her reputation for both quick action and bravery. According to the version of events she put in her autobiography—a version often repeated as true in the years since—it happened in the spring of 1877. Jane was riding toward the settlement of Crook City when she encountered an overland stagecoach that was being pursued by a group of American Indians. Calamity Jane rode up to the coach and realized that the driver was badly wounded. She jumped on, took the reins, and brought its half-dozen passengers safely into Deadwood.

This is just one of the many good stories told about Jane that have either been heavily embellished or are simply untrue. Evidence has emerged indicating that Jane could only have heard about this incident, not taken part in it, for the simple reason that she was not near Deadwood at the time. Furthermore, there is no mention

Calamity's Dress of Many Colors

Calamity Jane was never one to worry too much about her looks or about what people thought of them—and she was not shy about telling people what she thought when they dared to criticize or make fun of her.

Typical of this is the story of something that happened on one of her many trips—a stagecoach ride to Douglas, Wyoming. Wyoming historian Alfred Mokler, quoted in James D. McLaird's *Calamity Jane: The Woman and the Legend*, reports: "As was her custom, she had with her a plentiful supply of whisky, which she drank as she traveled along the rough road, to wash the dust from her throat and at the same time lend cheer and courage to endure the jolts of the rickety, rocking stage coach."

Jane also had with her a basket of grapes to snack on. She was wearing a dress with a pattern of red flowers, and as the coach forded the Platte River the dress got wet. Its colors ran, and once the journey got underway again she became covered with dust. When they arrived, Mokler comments, "Jane, with her dress of many colors, with her face and hands besmeared with grime and grape juice, with bedraggled hair, bleared eyes and sunburnt face, was a spectacle that caused many men to surround her and pass remarks not considered complimentary or pleasing to the new arrival." Jane's response, according to Mokler, "need not go down in history."

of the brave rescue in any newspaper of the time—an unthinkable turn of events for such a noteworthy story.

On the other hand, there is proof that during this time Jane revealed her unexpectedly tender side, in sharp contrast to her hell-raising reputation. Calamity Jane was never one to fuss much about her own health. However, the frontierswoman quickly gained a reputation in Deadwood for being the first to help others out when they were taken ill.

In her book *Calamity Jane*, Sollid quotes an article that appeared in the *Deadwood Pioneer* in July 1876, soon after Jane hit town that supports this. The newspaper noted: "The man Warren, who was stabbed on lower Main St. Wednesday night, is doing quite well under the care of Calamity Jane, who has kindly undertaken the job of nursing him. There's lots of humanity in Calamity, and she is deserving of much praise for the part she has taken in this particular case."

THE DEATH OF WILD BILL

Early in her stay in Deadwood, Calamity Jane's acquaintance with Wild Bill Hickok met an abrupt end—as did his life. On August 2, 1876, while playing poker at a table in Nuttall and Mann's No. 10 Saloon, Wild Bill was murdered.

His killer was a small-time drifter from Kentucky named Jack "Crooked Nose" McCall. Some historians have suggested that Mc-Call was hired to kill Hickok by criminals who feared that Wild Bill was going to be appointed marshal. However, there is no evidence to support this theory. The real reason for the murder was probably nothing more serious than an insult.

The day before, at the No. 10, a drunken McCall had steadily lost at a poker game that had also included Hickok. Wild Bill grew weary of McCall's unpleasant company, especially when he realized that McCall could no longer cover his losses. The gambler gave the drunken man some money, telling him to go away and get something to eat. Hickok further advised McCall not to return until he could cover his gambling debts. McCall took this dismissal as a grievous insult.

The next day, Hickok sat down again at the No. 10's poker table. He was unable to face the door, as was his custom while playing poker, so that he could watch out for enemies. Reluctantly, he sat with his back to the entrance. McCall, still smarting from the insult and probably sitting at his usual table by the door, managed to sneak up behind Hickok and shoot him in the head with a single-action .45 revolver. The killer then fled.

Hickok died instantly. It was later found that the gambler was holding aces and eights, and ever since that particular hand has been known as the Dead Man's Hand.

According to her autobiography, Jane was not present when Hickok was killed. When she heard the news, she wrote that she was in such a hurry that she did not take her guns with her. Instead, she tracked McCall to the town's butcher shop, where the killer was trying to hide, and attacked him with a meat cleaver.

Whether or not that part of the story is true, McCall was quickly taken into custody. On the same day of Hickok's funeral—an event that was attended by virtually the entire town—a jury was formed to try the murderer. McCall acknowledged that he had shot Hickok, but he claimed that it was justified revenge. "Crooked Nose" McCall swore that the gambler had killed his brother some time before in Abilene, Kansas.

For reasons that have never been fully understood, the jury found McCall not guilty after less than two hours of deliberation. Many people in the region ridiculed this blatantly unjust verdict. A piece in the local paper is a case in point. It is cited in an anonymous article in *Deadwood* magazine called "Wild Bill Cashed in His Last Chip in Deadwood." The editorial wryly commented: "Should it ever be our misfortune to kill a man . . . we would simply ask that our trial may take place in some of the mining camps of these hills."

After McCall was freed he quickly fled to Wyoming, allegedly bragging to people there that he had beaten Hickok in a fair fight. His liberty did not last long, however. Within a month, authorities ruled that McCall's trial had no legal basis, since the town of Deadwood was Indian Territory not on American soil.

The Wyoming government ruled that McCall should be retried. He was arrested in Laramie late in August and transported to Yankton, in what is now South Dakota. He was found guilty and was hanged the following spring—the first person to be executed by U.S. authorities in Dakota Territory.

THE AFTERMATH OF WILD BILL'S DEATH

Not surprisingly, the death of Will Bill was a devastating blow to Calamity Jane. Clearly, he had been the love of her life—even if he

Calamity Jane was devastated by the murder of Wild Bill Hickok. Jane reported in her autobiography that she went after Hickok's murderer with a meat cleaver, but this was later shown to be unlikely. Here, Jane is pictured at the grave of Wild Bill Hickok.

did not reciprocate her feelings. By all accounts, Jane sank into a deep depression after the murder and drank even more heavily than before.

Jane's deep grief is perfectly understandable. What is perhaps surprising is that she chose to stay in Deadwood. Not only did the town evoke bad memories for her, but it was unusual for her to stay so long in one place.

Nonetheless, she remained in or near town through the fall of 1876. During this time, she continued to work sporadically at a variety of jobs, including prospecting for gold. She also apparently rode a Pony Express route between Deadwood and Custer, a 50-mile

(80.5-km) journey that took her along one of the roughest trails in the Black Hills. In her autobiography, Calamity Jane wrote:

> As many of the riders before me had been held up and robbed of their packages, mail and money that they carried … it was considered the most dangerous route in the Hills, but as my reputation as a rider and quick shot was well known, I was molested very little, for the toll gatherers looked on me as being a good fellow, and they knew that I never missed my mark. I made the round trip every two days which was considered pretty good riding in that country.

It is a reasonable assumption that, like many people, Jane used hard work to help cope with her heartache in the months after Hickok's death. She also resumed her practice of helping others in need, although she could never completely abandon her rough ways. In "Calamity Jane—Rowdy Woman of the West," an article by Kathy Weiser on the Web site *Legends of America*, Deadwood's doctor is quoted as stating that as Jane tended to the sick, "she'd swear to beat hell at them, but it was a tender kind of cussin.'"

In the autumn of 1876, for instance, she helped nurse a miner named Jack McCarthy. McCarthy had broken his leg and, since he lived alone in a remote cabin, needed help to recover. According to several sources, Jane raised money for him by working in a dance hall, talked others into contributing as well, and purchased supplies for the injured miner. She arranged for these supplies to be packed out to his cabin and stayed there to care for him.

THE SMALLPOX EPIDEMIC

Calamity Jane also put in long weeks nursing the victims of a smallpox epidemic in and near Deadwood. According to some sources, eight Deadwood men suffered from this devastating (and often deadly) disease. They were quarantined in a shack in the nearby White Rock Mountains. An anonymously written article, "Martha

Jane 'Calamity Jane' Cannary," mentions this on the Web site *Women in History* (which is maintained by the Lakewood, Ohio, public library). In it, Calamity Jane's friend Dora DuFran, the madam of Deadwood's leading brothel, recalled about Jane, "[H]er good nursing brought five of these men out of the shadow of death, and many more later on, before the disease died out."

Other sources say that the outbreak of disease affected hundreds of people in the region, including many children. However many people were stricken, it is clear that Jane's efforts to care for them were extensive. She was apparently forced to improvise medicine for them, since she had only Epsom salts and cream of tartar to use. Not all of her patients lived. According to DuFran, Jane knew only one prayer, "Now I Lay Me Down to Sleep," which she would recite after burying any of her patients who did not survive.

Another account of the smallpox epidemic comes from Estelline Bennett, who grew up as the daughter of a territorial judge in the region. In her book *Old Deadwood Days*, quoted in Sollid's *Calamity Jane*, Bennett recalled that

> Calamity Jane alone took care of the smallpox patients in a crude log cabin pesthouse up in Spruce Gulch around behind White Rocks, the tall limestone peak over which the belated morning sun shines down on Deadwood Gulch. Smallpox was the most dreaded scourge of the frontier town. Usually people died because of dearth of nursing, of facilities for taking care of the sick, and bad sanitary conditions. For the same reasons, it spread with terrifying speed. Those who recovered came from their sick beds with marred faces. All that a town like Deadwood in '78 knew to do for smallpox patients was to set aside an isolated cabin and notify the doctor.
>
> There were half a dozen patients in the small log pesthouse in Spruce Gulch when Dr. Babcock made his first visit....[He] believed that without [Jane's] care not one of them would have pulled through.

Once the smallpox emergency was over, Jane's obligations to the sick came to an end. She regained her restlessness and decided to leave Deadwood.

One of Calamity Jane's first destinations after leaving town was Bear Butte Creek, not far from Deadwood. She apparently accompanied the 7th Cavalry there during 1878–1879, which was on assignment to help build the army outpost that eventually became known as Fort Meade. In her autobiography Jane claimed that she worked as a scout for the 7th Cavalry during this time, although that is open to speculation.

Also open to speculation are the details of Calamity Jane's travels in the years after her stay at Fort Meade. Reports of her whereabouts were spotty, although it is apparent that she was on the move constantly.

Despite stories to the contrary, there is no hard evidence that during this time she traveled much beyond the Montana and Dakota territories, with occasional forays into Idaho, Wyoming, and surrounding regions. From this time until she neared death many years later, Calamity Jane would continue to wander the frontier.

5

WANDERING THE WEST

By this time, Calamity Jane's reputation was beginning to travel much farther than it had before—much farther, in fact, than she herself had ever gone. As a result, Jane was able to start enjoying a growing celebrity status beyond her own region.

She had been a well-known figure in her part of the Old West for some years, but it was not until this period in her life that she started to become known nationally. This widespread fame had already begun. This occurred in the fall of 1877, when her name first appeared in a dime novel.

Dime novels were small illustrated pamphlets. They were extremely popular entertainments of the time, as ever present as television or the movies are today. Especially popular titles could easily sell hundreds of thousands of copies.

As the name implies, dime novels were fiction—and inventive fiction at that. Action was all important in a successful dime novel, so every page was well stocked with exciting adventures, sensational thrills, and exhilarating dialogue. Daryl Jones, in his scholarly work *The Dime Novel Western*, writes: "Often the plot of the dime novel seems nothing more than a fast-paced [and] loosely connected sequence of fistfights, gunplay, and hairbreadth

"Diamond Dick, Jr.'s Mysterious Diagram," in No. 191 of this Library.

Entered According to Act of Congress, in the Year 1897, by Street & Smith, in the Office of the Librarian of Congress, Washington, D. C.

Entered as Second-class Matter in the New York, N. Y., Post Office.   Issued Weekly. Subscription Price, $2.50 per Year.   July 4, 1896.

No. 192.   Street & Smith, Publishers.   NEW YORK.   79 Rose St., N. Y.   5 Cents.

Wild Bill's Last Trail.

By NED BUNTLINE.

WILD BILL SHOUTED: "GIVE UP THAT HORSE OR DIE!"

In October 1877, having gained a reputation for her unconventional ways, Calamity Jane became one of the featured characters in the popular Deadwood Dick dime novels. Her actions and accomplishments were greatly exaggerated, and she began to be recognized everywhere as the "dime novel heroine." Still, her wild behavior remained unchanged.

escapes strung out interminably and tied together by a happy ending."

Dime novels frequently used real-life figures as both lead figures and supporting characters. In his biography of Calamity Jane, McLaird comments, "It was not uncommon for authors to use the names of actual western figures, such as Kit Carson, Wild Bill Hickok, Davy Crockett, and Buffalo Bill, but events in the dime novels usually were fictional. This was the case concerning Calamity Jane." Mentions of living people like this were made without the permission of the person involved, and typically without any payment either.

DEADWOOD DICK MAKES JANE FAMOUS

In time, Jane was a figure in many dime novels. One particular set of these books, far more than any others, gave a tremendous boost to Jane's reputation. This was a wildly popular series of 33 novels set in the Black Hills about a character named Deadwood Dick. The first of these, published in 1877, was called *Deadwood Dick, the Prince of the Road; or, The Black Rider of the Black Hills*. Deadwood Dick was a completely fictional character, invented by the author of the series, a Pennsylvania writer named Edward L. Wheeler. Others who figured in the stories, however, were real people—including Calamity Jane.

The character of Jane proved to be a popular one. As the series progressed, she emerged as a major figure in the books, serving as the heroic Deadwood Dick's faithful companion and sometime love interest. As such, she figured prominently in many of Wheeler's others books, which boasted sensational titles like *Deadwood Dick on Deck; or, Calamity Jane, the Heroine of Whoop-Up*. Another typical title was *Deadwood Dick's Doom; or, Calamity Jane's Last Adventure, a Tale of Death Notch*.

Still another dime novel dubbed its heroine "The White Devil of the Yellowstone," a nickname she apparently adopted and used herself.

Although Jane was featured in dime novels by other writers, Wheeler's were so widely read that, through them, readers across the country became as familiar with Jane's name as they were already with Kit Carson, Billy the Kid, Buffalo Bill, and other celebrated Western figures. Her reputation rapidly spread, and her name began cropping up in newspapers far from her home territory, citing her as one of the West's most colorful characters.

It is possible that many of the eager readers of dime novels did not realize that the frontierswoman who featured in them was a real person. Quoted in McLaird's biography, the *Cheyenne Daily Leader* noted that the real Jane was as colorful as her fictional counterpart. It stated: "[M]any people think Calamity Jane is a heated myth of the disordered brain of some penny-a-liner, but she is a reality, and the pen of a half crazy imagination is not needed to enhance her actual deeds."

As she became better known, journalists frequently sought the frontierswoman out for interviews. Calamity loved the attention, and she did what she could to foster her fame. She especially enjoyed making up exciting stories for the writers, who often seem to have believed every word.

For example, according to Jane's account, she spent time with gangs of bandits and personally took part in a series of daring robberies. A number of newspapers printed this as genuine, although there is no evidence to back it up, and a number of people who knew her stated that it was completely false.

Some journalists even wrote supposedly true accounts of her life without ever having met her. One of them, apparently, was Horatio N. Maguire, a printer, editor, and judge in Montana who wrote a promotional pamphlet about the Black Hills. He included in it a flamboyant account of what he said was Calamity Jane's remarkable career of "ruin and recklessness."

Maguire claimed that his portrait of Jane was taken from personal experience, although several historians doubt that he ever met her. In any event, newspapers around the country picked up his highly fanciful writings about her, printed them verbatim, and spread the stories even further.

Of course, Jane did what she could to live up to her increasing notoriety. On one occasion, for instance, she pulled into Cheyenne on one of her periodic travels. When she arrived, she went to the office of the local newspaper, *The Leader*.

According to the editor's account of the incident (noted in McLaird's book), the editor fled before Jane arrived, not wanting to meet her. In his absence, the frontierswoman made the office boy write a note: "Print in the LEADER that Calamity Jane, the child of the regiment and pioneer white woman of the Black Hills, is in Cheyenne, or I'll scalp you, skin you alive, and hang you to a telegraph pole. You hear me and don't you forget it. CALAMITY JANE."

CALAMITY JANE FALLS ILL

Returning to Deadwood in the summer of 1879, Jane—who had always prided herself on her robust health—fell seriously ill again, this time with what was diagnosed as "congestion of the bowels." While she was recuperating, the *Deadwood Times* editor wrote an article praising Calamity Jane for her many charitable acts toward others. He made a special note that Jane's kindness had earned her many solid true friends among the citizens of the Black Hills.

The paper also reported that many of Deadwood's citizens were genuinely concerned about her illness. According to the same article, a local man arranged to provide the funds for whatever she needed to recover—despite the fact, as the editor put it, that she was a rough character who regularly broke several of the Ten Commandments. Excerpted in McLaird's biography, the *Deadwood-Times* further noted that "the thinking portion of our people" did not mind.

> [She is] a rough diamond of the border. [M]any a man who has been stricken with disease, in the wild, unfrequented corners of the frontier where no woman but Calamity dared to penetrate, owe their lives to the tender care [she provided].... These are among the solid virtues

of Calamity Jane. These traits of character make Calamity solid with the good people of the west.

Fortunately, Jane fully recovered by the fall. When she was well enough, she resumed her constant travel, moving around by horse, wagon, and train. There were reports that she was seen during the winter in Cheyenne, Rapid City, and Sturgis. According to one Sturgis resident, she worked at a dance hall and sold a mining claim she owned there, using the proceeds to buy a ranch. However, given her restless nature, it seems unlikely that Jane would have been content with settling long enough to want land.

Several witnesses have stated that Jane also traveled at one point to Rawlins in the company of a scarlet lady nicknamed Cotton Tail. But Calamity Jane had always craved the bustling activity of a wide-open boomtown; the region's bigger towns, like Rawlins, Cheyenne, Rapid City, and now Deadwood were becoming too civilized and tame for her taste. Increasingly, Jane was drawn to Fort Pierre, in what is now central South Dakota. It was shaping up to be the latest of the region's boomtowns.

CALAMITY JANE BEHIND THE BAR

The reason for Fort Pierre's rapid growth was a similar story to those of many other towns: It was in the path of the railroad's direction as it moved west. According to her autobiography, Jane found occasional work there driving teams of horses and mules.

It appears that most of her time in Fort Pierre, however, was spent running a saloon. Running a noisy, crowded bar would have fit in well with Jane's personality. So would Fort Pierre's overall boisterous atmosphere, which was typical in its abundance of drinking, gambling, the occasional gun battle, and general excitement. So much drinking took place in Fort Pierre, one resident joked, that if the saloons were gone there would not be enough of the town left to sneeze at.

Nonetheless, Jane's place had rules. Its reputation was an establishment where no thievery or other mistreatment was allowed, and

Calamity Jane could out-fight, out-shoot, and out-drink many men. She drank so much of the "bug juice," as whiskey was called by some, and caused so much chaos after she drank that some bartenders banned her from their saloons. Here, Calamity Jane, in a seldom-worn dress, drinks with some men outside a bar in Giltedge, Montana.

the bar's strong-willed owner enforced the law. When bullwhackers and other laborers were done with their jobs, one Pierre resident recalled (he is quoted in McLaird's book), they "thought of 'Calam' and the good times they could have at her place in Pierre—where they wouldn't be robbed, overcharged, or mistreated."

McLaird's biography also cites Albert Lot Hamlin, who made a living in Fort Pierre building sheds in which to tan animal hides. Hamlin recalled how Jane looked while running her saloon: "Behind the bar she stood, about five foot nine inches high. She had dark brown eyes, high cheekbones. . .and a pointed chin. Her raven hair was tucked up under a brown Stetson hat. She was entirely garbed in buckskin—both trousers and coat and vest, a red bandanna around her neck. A small-sized pair of black high heel boots finished out her other extremity."

During her time in Fort Pierre, Calamity was again periodically called on to care for the sick. Those she helped included one elderly woman who said she would tolerate Jane's presence only if the "nurse" wore a dress and refrained from smoking, drinking, or cursing. Calamity Jane agreed and performed her duties for several weeks. As soon as the patient improved, Jane hit the bars and within an hour was so drunk, one observer remarked, that she would not have been able to hit the floor with her hat. Once again, Jane did not stay put for long. She went wandering again around 1881, this time dropping out of sight for about a year. The next documented evidence of her whereabouts came when she was spotted in Bismarck, North Dakota, and Miles City, Montana, early in 1882.

If her autobiography is to be believed, Jane traveled widely and spent some time operating a roadside ranch on the Yellowstone River in Montana Territory, "where the weary traveler could be accommodated with food, drink, or trouble if he looked for it." Some historians, however, feel that Jane did not travel as extensively as she claimed.

It is more likely, they argue, that she spent most of her missing year following the Northern Pacific railway line as it made its way west to meet another track being built from the West Coast. When these tracks met, at Garrison, Montana Territory, in the fall of 1883, they completed the first transcontinental railroad. This enormous feat of engineering and labor created a dramatic and permanent shift in the history of the Old West. It allowed massive numbers of settlers to advance west in relative safety, speed, and comfort, greatly accelerating the end of the frontier era.

As the rail link was nearing completion, Calamity Jane no doubt moved from town to town while doing her best to avoid the encroaching trappings of civilization. As always, she did whatever she could to earn a living. Her jobs likely included chopping wood, cooking, cleaning laundry, and working occasionally as a dance hall girl and at a brothel.

She was no more well behaved than she had ever been. As she moved around, Jane was allegedly involved in a number of disreputable events, including a horse-rustling scheme (although this was never proved). More certain is the fact that she was briefly arrested for illegally selling liquor to American Indians near the town of Missoula, Montana. Everywhere she went, people noted that Jane was always up to her old ways: She was still fond of gambling, chewing tobacco and smoking a cigar at the same time, swearing "like a man," and, of course, drinking.

During this time in Montana Territory, according to some newspaper reports, Calamity Jane gave birth to a son, whom she nicknamed "Little Calamity." The father may have been a cowboy named Frank Koenig or King who apparently lived with Jane for some time. (She supposedly sometimes went by the name Mattie King.) The baby did not live long, however, and Jane moved on again—minus King—to the western part of the territory.

She spent the winter of 1883–1884 in Montana's Yellowstone Valley, and spring found her in the town of Livingston. There, she allegedly took part in a staged prizefight with a saloonkeeper named Madam Bull Dog. According to this tale, the huge Madam Bull Dog overpowered Jane and was declared the winner—but the crowd's sympathies were with the underdog, and Calamity Jane was treated to drinks all night.

Later that spring, the frontierswoman headed west to Eagle City—another boomtown, this one built around a gold strike in the Coeur d'Alene region of northern Idaho. Gold had been discovered there in the winter of 1882–1883, and by the spring of 1884 an estimated 200 would-be prospectors and others hoping for work were arriving every day.

JANE ON THE STAGE

It is possible that in Eagle City, Idaho, Jane made the first of what would become many stage appearances. Adam Aulbach, the editor of the *Coeur d'Alene Sun*, wrote in his paper in 1884 about a stage production he witnessed, which he described as the first significant social event in Eagle City. It took place in a tent that served as a bar-room, where whiskey cost 15 cents a shot and "games of chance" were available.

The star of the show, Aulbach related, was Calamity Jane. To the accompaniment of four fiddlers, as the show began, curtains parted to reveal her wearing male clothing. She narrated a monologue of her life, after which "the party was on." Quoted in McLaird's book, Aulbach continued:

> A dance was announced. The eight girls were lined up at the end of the long tent. The excess of Beau Brummells wishing to dance made a routine imperative. Each male was allowed a choice and one turn around the dance floor, then another partner took over. . . .
>
> Short tempers! Fights! The crimson silhouettes on the snow attested to this. The bouncers gave much to their manly art. Then inertia. Night became day, the hanging lamps cast a ghastly dull glow. The party was over.
>
> Calamity said goodbye in her inimitable way—a rough-housing push, a shake and a hug. She yelled above the din: "At least we ain't cooking in the hot boxes of hell. . . . I'll be back when the birds are atwittering in the spring."

There is evidence that during this period Jane appeared else-where on stage, telling tales of her exploits and otherwise enter-taining eager audiences. If so, this was with a traveling Wild West program called the Great Rocky Mountain Show. However, this story may not be accurate. The "Calamity Jane" who appeared with this show may have been an imposter.

Imposter or not, the performer was one of the troupe's stars, along with Curley, an American Indian advertised as the only survivor of Custer's Last Stand, and a legendary mountain man named John "Liver-Eating" Johnson (who got his name because he supposedly hated Crow Indians so much that he killed every one he saw and took a bite from the body's liver). According to one source, this show ran out of money in the Midwest, and the troupe had to sell its horses to pay for its return to the West.

CALAMITY JANE TAKES A HUSBAND. . . . MAYBE

Calamity's exact travels after she left Eagle City in 1884 are unclear. She was seen sporadically around her usual haunts in the Montana and Dakota territories, and she wrote in her autobiography that she also visited California, Texas, and Arizona during this period. By all accounts, Jane was her usual self wherever she went. Quoted in Sollid's *Calamity Jane*, the *Laramie Boomerang* reported in February 1887: "To say that the old girl has reformed is somewhat of a chestnut [tired joke]. She was gloriously drunk this morning and if she didn't make Rome howl she did Laramie. Her resting place is now the soft side of an iron cell. Judge Pease will deliver the lecture and collect the fine in [the] morning."

Another of Jane's stories in her autobiography is that she married a man named Clinton Burke in Texas in 1885. Her reason for marrying, she wrote, was that "I thought I had traveled through life long enough alone and thought it was about time to take a partner for the rest of my days." Some researchers guess that they actually met later, perhaps in the fall of 1891.

Even if the date of their meeting is unclear, Jane definitely was romantically linked with Burke, off and on, for some years. However, there is no evidence that they formally married. It was fairly common and accepted in the Old West for couples to live together in what was called a common-law marriage.

According to some sources, over the years Calamity was also romantically linked with several other men, including Robert Dorsett and Charles Townley, about whom little is known. But the most significant of these attachments was a stormy and occasionally violent relationship with a railway brakeman named Bill Steers.

Beginning in 1893, Calamity Jane joined several Wild West shows, including her old friend Buffalo Bill's show. She traveled around the country as a horse rider and trick shooter, but her alcoholism caused problems and she was fired. Here is Calamity Jane on horseback in 1901 during her days as a Wild West performer.

It appears that at some point during this period Calamity Jane gave birth to a daughter named Jessie. If this is true, it is likely that Steers was the father. However, Jane repeatedly claimed later in life that Wild Bill Hickok was the father; meanwhile, it is certainly possible that the girl's father was someone else entirely.

Calamity Jane herself said that Jessie was born on October 28, 1887. According to McLaird's book, Jane told a reporter in 1896, "She's all I've got to live fer; she's my only comfort." There has been speculation that Jessie may have had a different natural mother and that Jane informally adopted her. In any case, it is true that a girl lived and traveled with Jane for years, and Jane called the girl her daughter. For his part, McLaird, Calamity's most reputable biographer, believes that she was indeed Jessie's mother.

Some evidence backs up stories Calamity told about adventures in the late 1880s and early 1890s; others do not. According to some sources, including her autobiography, Jane and her new husband, Burke, ran a hotel in Boulder, Colorado, between 1889 and 1893. Then, abandoning her husband, she took a job with Buffalo Bill's Wild West Show as a horse rider and trick shooter.

There are strong indications, however, that during this period she instead spent significant time near Fort Washakie, in the Wind River country of Wyoming. She may have been there to follow the growth of boomtowns as the Burlington railway was built through northeast Wyoming. According to one report, she was also spotted in the silver-mining boomtown of Creede, Colorado.

Wherever she showed up, Jane was always newsworthy and could be counted on for a colorful interview. McLaird's biography quotes a reporter who spoke with her late in 1889 in Wendover, Wyoming. The journalist wrote:

> Calamity is one of the most amiable of women; ornery [sic] of feature though kindly of eye, and an enthusiastic [fan of] the whisky market. Her manner betrays an unstrung and emotional temperament.... But there are many worse people in the world than Old Calamity. As a female holy terror she has no living superior, and her worst enemies will not deny that she is an able drinker.

Calamity Jane also surfaced in Omaha, Nebraska, in February 1892. According to a newspaper reporter there, she was on her way to visit her sister in Iowa. The Omaha article repeated many of the stories about Jane that were becoming firmly entrenched in her public persona: that she had been a scout for the U.S. Army and had carried important messages for the military; that she had killed

The Portrait of Calamity Jane

According to legend, while Jane was spending some time in Billings, Montana Territory, a painter arrived in town from the West Coast. He did not drink, but he did spend time in saloons, painting portraits of customers. When he met Calamity in one of the town's bars, he liked her face and asked if he could paint her.

She agreed, but only if he matched her drink for drink. Before they started, the painter made sure she had already been drinking hard. Then, as he worked, the painter kept pretending to drop his brush. Each time he did this, he secretly poured his drink into a nearby spittoon. This made it seem that he was matching her drink for drink as he worked.

Unfortunately, there is no way to prove the truth of this story. The painting was allegedly destroyed in a fire—if it ever existed in the first place.

40 American Indians and 17 white men; and that she had narrowly escaped from dozens of assassination attempts and other deadly situations.

BACK HOME TO THE BLACK HILLS

In the summer of 1894, Jane was spotted at the Fourth of July celebration in the small Montana town of Cinnabar. (Montana was by now a state, having been admitted in 1889.) Ida McPherren, a resident of Cinnabar, is quoted in McLaird's book recalling Jane's appearance there: She was "dressed in buckskin trousers, fringed buckskin jacket and a man's wide brimmed hat; in the height of her glory because she was creating a sensation."

Then it was on to other points, including Billings and Sheridan. In Miles City, she ran afoul of the law—the exact reason is unknown—and had to flee to avoid $100 fine and jail time. According to some reports, Clinton Burke, the man she may have married in Texas, was with her for at least part of this time.

Jane was also seen in Crawford, Nebraska, near Fort Robinson. It is likely that she was once again traveling through a succession of boomtowns, following a railway under construction. In this case, it was the Fremont, Elkhorn & Missouri Valley Railroad as it made its way toward Wyoming. She probably lived in a tent during her stay in Crawford, as did most people in these instantly created towns.

Stories told about Calamity during this period attest to her continued kindness toward strangers. One Crawford resident recalled the time Jane took up a collection after a young stranger was killed in a blasting-powder accident. The money paid for his funeral, as well as for finding his parents and shipping his remains home.

By 1894 or 1895 (sources differ), Jane was back in her beloved Black Hills. When she hit Deadwood, the event was trumpeted in the Black Hills *Daily Times,* in an article that described Calamity (perhaps sarcastically, given how well people there knew her) as a fearless Indian fighter and rover of the plains.

It was her first visit in about 15 years to the town. In the intervening years, Deadwood had dramatically calmed down and changed from its rowdy beginnings. Nonetheless, Calamity Jane was pleased to be there. She was getting older, and her hard life was taking a toll on her health.

Not everyone in the Black Hills was happy to see her again. Nonetheless, many of her old friends in Deadwood recalled her liveliness and her kindness toward the sick, and these people greeted her with pleasure. Calamity Jane was even invited to use the sheriff's office as a place in which she could spend time with friends. In her autobiography, she wrote: "My arrival in Deadwood after an absence of so many years created quite an excitement among my many friends of the past, to such an extent that a vast number of the citizens who had come to Deadwood during my absence who had heard so much of Calamity Jane and her many adventures in former years were anxious to see me."

At first the "old girl," as her friends affectionately called her, seemed less rambunctious than her earlier self. The newspaper in Deadwood noted that, thanks to the hard life she had led, Jane looked poorly and showed few traces of her former spirit.

Her manner was markedly quieter; most of the time she dressed not in buckskin but in a worn black dress and coat. She told everyone that she wanted to find regular work, and hoped to send her daughter to school. In the meantime, she was able to make a little money and obtain credit at the general store by selling photos of herself.

Although Jane continued to travel periodically, she remained primarily in the Deadwood area—the region she thought of the most as home—during her final years.

CALAMITY JANE'S FINAL YEARS

Despite her intentions to lead a less rowdy life in Deadwood, Calamity often reverted to her old ways. She continued to drink and smoke, and she was still quick to become belligerent when challenged. Also, although Jane loved her daughter, she was not as responsible toward Jessie as she could have been.

According to legend, for instance, the citizens of Deadwood held a fund-raiser to send Jessie to a convent school in Sturgis, South Dakota, in an effort to provide a better atmosphere for the girl. Jane, however, was unable to resist spending all of the donated money immediately. She blew it on treating her friends to drinks one night. At the end of the evening, so the story goes, she paraded up and down the streets singing at the top of her lungs. Dora DuFran found her asleep on Main Street and had to help her home.

Soon after Jane's return to Deadwood, a female newspaper reporter, M.L. Fox, interviewed her. Calamity was temporarily living in her friend California Jack's home when the meeting took place.

Quoted in McLaird's book, Fox described the place as "a cozy little house set among the pines." Despite its snug looks, however, Jane apologized for the untidy state of both the house and herself: "Walk right in. Rather dirty-lookin' house, but we've been 'bout sick an' let things go. I ain't combed my head today; looks like it, too, I 'spose."

Despite Calamity's opinion of her own looks, Fox described the celebrity as having a striking appearance. Jane, the journalist wrote, was "of medium height, robust, rather inclined to stoutness, and looks to be in the prime of her life, but I believe she is past that, though her hair, which is long, still retains its natural brown color; her eyes are dark gray, and their expressions are many. Her chin is firm and mouth decided."

Calamity's daughter Jessie, who had been attending the local school, came home from class while Fox was still visiting. The reporter described the girl, who was about nine years old, as being neatly dressed and shy, with a bright face and good manners despite any shortcomings in her upbringing.

RETURNING TO THE STAGE

Soon after she arrived back in Deadwood, it became clear that Jane was eager to return to performing on stage. She had been sending out letters for some time, hoping to obtain a contract with a show business troupe.

In her autobiography, Calamity stated that these letters met with great success. According to her, among the many people she met in Deadwood "were several gentlemen from eastern cities who advised me to allow myself to be placed before the public in such a manner as to give the people of the eastern cities an opportunity of seeing the Woman Scout who was made so famous through her daring career in the West and Black Hill countries."

She agreed to sign up with a troupe called the Diamond Dick & Company Wild West Show. However, when the time came, she failed to arrive for an appointment with the organizers and the deal fell through.

More successful was an engagement with the Kohl & Middleton chain of dime museums. Dime museums were institutions in large cities that were very popular at the time. The famous entrepreneur P.T. Barnum founded the first of these attractions. They

The Dog-Faced Man.

KOHL & MIDDLETON'S
South Side Dime Museum,
MONDAY, MARCH 2d.
(See Other Side)

Calamity Jane earned money by selling photos of herself and working as an attraction at Kohl and Middleton's dime museum. Her first show was with the Palace Museum in Minneapolis in 1896. This poster announces the appearance of the "Dog-Faced Man" at the South Side Dime Museum.

featured a variety of curiosities, exotic animals, educational lectures, and other entertainments.

Jane agreed to appear several times a day in her own show, reciting a monologue about her adventures and displaying some of her shooting abilities. She had to sign a contract promising not to swear; the audiences included women and children, so the material needed to be clean. Jane also agreed to hold her drinking to a minimum.

Calamity's initial contract with Kohl & Middleton called for an eight-week engagement in four cities, at a fee of $50 per week plus expenses. This was good money, at least for someone like Jane. It was a much better salary than she could have earned at her usual occupations. In addition to the salary she drew for her performances, Calamity was allowed to sell copies of her autobiography to audiences.

Clinton Burke was offered a job with the troupe as well, and he accompanied his wife when she left Deadwood. How the couple arranged to care for Jessie during this period is unknown. However, it is unlikely that she traveled with them. It is more probable that she stayed in Deadwood or Sturgis with friends so that she could continue her schooling.

ON THE ROAD

To prepare for her tour, Calamity had a fancy Western outfit made, including black cowboy boots with three-inch heels. She also practiced shooting a rifle, something she had not done for a long time. Jane traveled to Minneapolis, Minnesota, for her debut appearance in January 1896. Sollid's book *Calamity Jane* quotes an advertisement for this show:

> The famous woman scout of the Wild West. Heroine of a thousand thrilling adventures. The terror of evil-doers in the Black Hills! The comrade of Buffalo Bill and Wild Bill Hickok. See this famous woman and hear

On Her Flying Steed

This excerpt from the 1885 book *Deadwood Dick on Deck or, Calamity Jane: The Heroine of Whoop-Up*, by E.L. Wheeler, is reprinted in *Cowgirls: Women of the American West* by Teresa Jordan. It is a perfect example of the overheated prose that the dime novels of the day and how it was used to portray Calamity Jane's exciting adventures:

> She dashed madly down through the gulch one day, standing erect upon the back of her unsaddled cayuse, and the animal running at the top of its speed, leaping sluices and other obstructions—still the dare-devil retained her position as if glued to the animal's back, her hair flowing wildly back from beneath her slouch hat, her eyes dancing occasionally with excitement, as she recognized some wondering pilgrim, every now and then her lips giving vent to a ringing whoop, which was creditable in imitation if not in volume and force to that of a full-blown Comanche warrior.
>
> Now, she dashed away through the narrow gulch, catching with delight long breaths of the perfume of flowers which met her nostrils at every onward leap of her horse, piercing the gloom of the night with her dark lovely eyes, searchingly lest she should be surprised; lighting a cigar at full motion-dashing on, on, this strange girl of the Hills went, on her flying steed.

her graphic descriptions of her daring exploits. A Host of Other Attractions. A Big Stage Show. That's All—A Dime—That's all!

Jane's appearances, by all accounts, were successful. She drew large crowds and was apparently able to keep her drinking, cursing, and bad behavior in check. After her engagement in Minneapolis, Jane continued to Chicago, where her arrival was front-page news. By this point Burke was no longer with her, for unknown reasons.

The "famous woman scout" still loved to talk to reporters wherever she went, embellishing her stories without modesty. These newspapermen dutifully recorded the tall tales that Calamity Jane told about her adventures. When asked what she hoped to do in their city, Jane told reporters that she longed to ride a bucking bronco in the streets and shoot coyotes in the suburbs.

Not everyone in the East was satisfied with Jane's appearances, however. Reporters in some cities noted that many people in the audience expressed disappointment that she was such an ordinary-looking woman. They had expected something more exotic from the famous Calamity Jane.

The rest of Jane's tour with the Kohl & Middleton organization probably took her to Philadelphia, Pennsylvania, and to New York City. There is some evidence that the engagement was extended to include Cincinnati, Ohio, as well. She stayed on the tour circuit until the end of May before heading back west.

After returning to Deadwood, Jane picked up Jessie and went on the move again. After a brief stop in Newcastle, Wyoming, mother and daughter continued on to Montana. Burke apparently joined them there for a time, but he and Jane again quarreled and separated. He then returned to Deadwood.

Mother and daughter remained in Montana, visiting a series of settlements there, including Helena, Anaconda, and Castle. Jane apparently intended to stay for a while in Castle. She started a restaurant and enrolled Jessie in school.

After a few weeks, however, Calamity Jane was arrested for failing to pay a man for a team of horses. The case probably was settled out of court, since there are no records of fines or jail time incurred. Jane and Jessie moved on to Billings and then Yellowstone National Park, where Jane earned a few dollars by selling pictures of herself to tourists.

After that, there is no hard evidence of Jane's whereabouts until June of 1898. Some sources say she made a second dime museum tour during this period, but there is no proof of this.

NORTH TO THE YUKON

In any case, the next public mention of her came from a place far from her characteristic home turf: the town of Dawson, in the Yukon Territory of far northwest Canada. Jane had come to this snowbound land to take part in one of the biggest gold-mining stampedes in history: the massive Klondike gold rush.

Gold had been discovered in the Yukon in the fall of 1896. A rush of prospectors descended almost immediately. These would-be miners came from as far away as Europe, South Africa, and Australia, primarily passing through West Coast ports such as Seattle and San Francisco. Spurring them on was the promise of riches in the midst of a serious economic depression.

Typically, they made the arduous trek north by sailing up the Inside Passage and landing at Skagway, in what was then Alaska Territory. From there, the route took them on foot along the 33-mile (53-km) Chilkoot Trail. Each would-be miner carried with him a ton of supplies, enough to last through an entire winter.

This route required climbing an especially dangerous pass. Some 1,500 steps were carved out of snow and ice; the trail was only 2 feet (0.61 m) wide at some points, with a 500-foot (152-m) drop if a foot was misplaced. Since the Chilkoot Pass was too steep for packhorses to navigate, miners had to leave some of their supplies along the way, returning periodically to move it piecemeal up the mountain.

Some miners needed a little help to make it over the summit. A reporter for *Leslie's Weekly* magazine, quoted on arcticwebsite.com, wrote home in 1897: "There is a spot on the Chilkoot Pass where the grade is so steep that progression is easiest on all fours, and . . . a brisk gate [sic] is best attained when an Indian propels the traveler by butting him with his head from behind."

Navigating this pass was just the beginning of the overland journey. From there it was another 500 miles (805 km) by river to reach Dawson City. Despite the hardships and dangers, however, by the summer of 1898 an estimated 100,000 people had started the trek. Of them only about 30,000 made it all the way; the rest died

Word spread quickly when gold was first discovered in Canada's Yukon River valley in 1896. Prospectors hauled a year's worth of supplies through thick snow and treacherous ice and over dangerous Chilkoot Pass, which was given the nickname "the meanest 32 miles in the world."

or simply gave up and turned back. Jane was one of the successful ones.

The *Klondike Nugget*, Dawson's newspaper, announced Calamity Jane's arrival in its issue of June 23. Adding a new twist to Jane's fanciful list of accomplishments—that she had been a detective for a large stagecoach transport company—the newspaper wrote:

> Calamity Jane, of Deadwood and Leadville fame, and one of Wells-Fargo's most trusted detectives, is in Dawson. The life of this woman has been filled with wild adventures, and on more than one occasion she has been forced to take human life in defense of her own; yet a kinder, truer character would be hard to find.

In upholding the law and defending what is right, she
is braver than most men, she is gentle and refined as any
of her Eastern sisters. There is a suggestion in the steel-
blue eyes, however, that would warn the unwary, and a
glance at the half-sad face indicates that her life has not
been all sunshine.

Despite all of the obvious trouble and hardships that she went
through in order to reach Dawson, Jane apparently spent only a few
weeks there. The reason for this is unknown. Some historians have
speculated that there were too many people already staking claims
there. It might have been too difficult for late arrivals like Jane to
make money.

On the other hand, Jane always had an ability to make money in
even the roughest circumstances, so that may not be a valid reason.
Perhaps she simply disliked it, and her lifelong restlessness kicked
in again.

Whatever the reason, Calamity Jane was back in Montana by
the late summer of 1898. She and Jessie, who had probably been left
with friends, spent the next several years in the state, moving from
town to town. At one point, in Billings for a relatively long spell, Jane
reenrolled Jessie in school and found work in laundries, as a cook
and ranch hand, or in any other capacity she could find.

WORN OUT AND WEARY

By now, Jane's hard life—her long years of heavy drinking and
carousing—were starting to take a genuinely serious toll. According to those who knew or interviewed her, Jane was worn out and
weary—she was only in her mid-forties, but appeared much older.
One reporter cited in McLaird's biography described Calamity
Jane during this time, noting that her tired-looking face was at
odds with her still-spirited walk: "Her deeply-lined, scowling,
sun-tanned face and the mouth and its missing teeth might have
belonged to a hag of seventy. [When she walked, however, she

looked like] a thirty-year-old cowpuncher just coming into town for his night to howl."

Jane had always prided herself on her robust health and her ability to thrive in even the roughest conditions. Now, however, her physical strength began to fail. In 1901, while on a train near the town of Livingston, she fell ill. After being taken off the railroad car, witnesses said, Jane was confused and told them she had no money. She was taken to the poorhouse and examined by a doctor, who did not feel her illness was serious.

Jane recovered fairly quickly. Still, the news that she had been forced to live in the poorhouse was reported in local papers. The fact that she was in this shameful situation embarrassed even Jane, not a woman who was ever noted for

In Calamity Jane's later years, she was broke and appeared much older than her actual age. Her attempts to sell her autobiography and earn enough money to retire were unsuccessful, and she did not have many other prospects except to survive by taking in laundry and cooking for others.

caring what others thought of her. On the other hand, the knowledge becoming public had its benefits. Friends and acquaintances, touched by reports about the famous woman's troubles, sent her money.

Calamity Jane moved on, only to fall ill again. In May of 1901, she was found incapacitated in the back of Taft's Saloon in Red Lodge, Montana. A doctor was summoned, arrangements made for her care, and a friend promised to tend to her. Jane did not take advantage of this, however; she left abruptly and boarded another train. Calamity Jane's already remarkable life then took a strange turn.

ENTER JOSEPHINE BRAKE, JOURNALIST

The news that Jane was ill and broke came to the attention of a writer on the East Coast named Josephine Brake. Brake had apparently been intrigued for some time by Calamity Jane's story and notoriety. The writer decided to rescue her.

Several possible reasons for this have been proposed. Some historians believe that Brake was acting unselfishly, wanting only to help a famous figure who was down on her luck. According to this scenario, Brake wanted to bring Jane back east and let her live the rest of her years in comfort, perhaps with the aid of a government pension. (In those days, there was nothing like Social Security to aid older people, but government pensions were sometimes awarded.)

Strong evidence, however, shows that Brake's reasons were less noble. This evidence indicates that Brake had been enlisted to tempt Jane back into public performances, and that the journalist hoped to become the celebrity's manager and thus benefit financially. The public show that Brake apparently represented would be part of a huge world's fair, the Pan-American Exposition, in Buffalo, New York.

Whatever her reasons may have been for coming to Montana, Brake arrived in July and found Jane ill, recuperating in the hut of an African-American woman on the banks of the Yellowstone. On July 12, 1901, the *Buffalo News* ran a story headlined: "Calamity Jane to End Her Days in Buffalo." (The article appears on "Pan American Exposition 1901," a Web site maintained by the *News*.) The article continued:

> Mrs. Josephine Winfield Brake, of Buffalo, N.Y., author
> and newspaper correspondent, has been in Montana for

the past week searching for "Calamity Jane," the plains-woman. Yesterday Mrs. Brake discovered . . . the poor woman. The scene that followed the offer of Mrs. Brake to take Calamity to her own home in Buffalo, where she could spend the remainder of her days in comfort, was pathetic in the extreme and the noted frontierswoman wept like a child.

Jane did go east with Brake, although sources differ as to whether Jane willingly accepted the offer. Meanwhile, reaction to this turn of events was mixed. The Billings newspaper printed a headline frankly stating the editor's opinion that Calamity Jane was leaving Montana in dubious company.

Many of her friends also worried that Brake intended to take advantage of Jane. Why, they wondered, would someone who had never met Jane travel so far to rescue her? Was Jane really being rescued? How could Brake afford to keep Jane in comfort, as she promised? And how well would Jane do, far from the region where she had spent most of her life?

As a result of these concerns, many people in Montana and elsewhere predicted that the trip would be a disaster. Sure enough, by the time they reached Minnesota tension had arisen between the two. According to a reporter in St. Paul, Brake was visibly nervous and admitted that life with Jane was not easy. For one thing, for some reason Jane refused to speak with interviewers. Also, she had agreed to drink only when Brake approved, but was so unpleasant when she was sober that the chaperone frequently allowed her to drink as a way to keep things calm.

Despite these difficulties, the pair did reach Buffalo and connect with the fair's organizer, a flamboyant entrepreneur named Colonel Fred Cummins. His giant exposition opened in May 1901. It featured such attractions as a new invention called the "X-ray machine"; leaders from 42 American Indian tribes of North America (the famous chief Geronimo had top billing); and one of the first examples of long-distance transmission of electricity. Among the fair's many celebrity visitors were U.S. president William McKinley—who was assassinated while attending it—and the man who succeeded him, Vice President Theodore Roosevelt.

Brake rented a house for Jane and Cummins signed her to a contract. Wearing her famous buckskins, Calamity Jane appeared in a parade, driving a cart with 100 mules, and was also part of a Wild West show that featured rifle shooting, Indian races, and a battle reenactment with 500 participants—all in an arena that seated an audience of 25,000.

Jane was a big hit, with thousands of visitors flocking to see her. However, much of the salary that the star should have gotten apparently never reached her. Instead, the money went to Brake. This naturally infuriated Jane, and their relations grew increasingly strained. Brake left the partnership, and Jane was able to strike a bargain with Cummins for more money.

TROUBLE AT THE FAIR

However, the new arrangement was not a success. The star began drinking heavily again, and her behavior grew increasingly aggressive. At one point, she was arrested by the Buffalo police and spent a night in jail for disorderly conduct (claiming all the while that it was the first time she had ever been arrested). Calamity Jane managed to get into other kinds of trouble as well; she fought with an exposition guard and fell in love with a local man named Frederick Darlington, leading to rumors that they might marry.

In time, her drinking, belligerence, and depression forced Cummins to fire her. In August, a newspaper story headlined "Alas, 'Calamity Jane'—the Aged Celebrity, Overcome by Liquor, Arrested, and Released on Suspended Sentence" and reprinted on the Web site of the *Buffalo News*, reported the performer's final offense:

> The original "Calamity Jane" of Wild West fame and who has been with the Indian Congress at the Exposition during the last month, spent last night behind prison bars.

Patrolman Charles P. Gore of the Austin Street Station found the old woman on Amherst Street, near the Exposition gate, last night. She was reeling from side to side and did not appear to know where she was. The woman had been drinking and Gore placed her under arrest.

She spent the night in the matron's custody at the Pearl Street Station, was taken before Judge Rochford this morning and released on suspended sentence.

Jane, unemployed and broke, needed funds to get home. When Buffalo Bill Cody's show arrived in Buffalo in late August, he lent his old friend the money for a ticket and food. Quoted in McLaird's book, Cody remarked to an interviewer that he was happy to help out someone from his Wild West past: "[N]one of us on the frontier ever met any one like her. . . . [T]here is no more frontier any more and never will be again, and that is why we like to look back, and why the few that remain of the old-timers we marched with and fought with have a warm place in our affections, whatever or wherever they may be."

CALAMITY JANE GOES HOME

By all accounts, the local police were happy to see her go. As free with her spending as always, however, she only traveled as far as Chicago before the money ran out. She got another job at a dime museum to raise enough funds to get to Minneapolis, and she continued in this way to slowly make her way back west. She was in Pierre, South Dakota, by November, where she stayed for about six months.

Not surprisingly, she found trouble there, including an arrest for stealing a bottle of whiskey. She also broke her ribs and was laid up for some time. A few sympathetic people gave her firewood and other supplies, and she holed up for the rest of the winter in a shack near Pierre, South Dakota.

In the spring of 1902, she made her way further west, encountering various old acquaintances as she traveled. Several of them later stated that they had a hard time recognizing Jane—her appearance had changed so much for the worse. Finally, after being away for nine months, Jane returned to the open skies, mountains, and prairies of Montana. Then, on her first night in Billings, she was arrested for being drunk and disorderly and spent the night in jail.

Billings was no longer the wide-open and tolerant town it had been in Jane's glory days, and it was no longer to her liking. She moved on and settled in Gardiner, Montana, north of Yellowstone National Park. While she was there, a thief tried to steal a ring that Jane said Wild Bill Hickok had given her. Still, Jane failed to appear at the thief's court appearance, and the judge was forced to release him.

While in Gardiner, Jane once again fell seriously ill. The county arranged to pay for her train passage to Livingston, where arrangements were made to commit her to the Park County Poor Farm. She refused to go, however, instead borrowing enough money for whiskey and a ticket to Lombard. Then she missed the train.

Calamity Jane was found asleep on a bench in front of a hotel and placed briefly back in the county jail. This time, she promised to leave town. A few weeks later, the frontierswoman was spotted by residents in two central Montana towns, Lewistown and Kendall, and probably remained in that region through the rest of the summer.

In the fall she headed back to Billings, although she was still in poor health. A handful of newspapers in the West and Midwest, along with some of her friends and supporters, had joined together in a campaign to secure a government pension for Calamity Jane. However, there was opposition to this plan from other papers and individuals, who stated that she was dissolute and unworthy of support despite her fame.

THE DEATH OF CALAMITY JANE

At some point in 1903, probably in early summer, Jane returned to the Black Hills. In the last stages of alcoholism, and carrying her few belongings in a battered suitcase, she arrived in the town of

Calamity Jane died on August 1, 1903, at the age of 51. She was given a hero's ceremony for her kindness during the smallpox epidemic and buried next to Wild Bill Hickok at Mount Moriah Cemetery in South Dakota.

Belle Fourche. The town, near the western border of South Dakota, had once been a center for gold mining, cattle shipping, and the fur trade.

There she rejoined her old friend Dora DuFran, who was running a brothel. An article in *Deadwood* magazine, "Girls of the Gulch," notes that the establishment was advertised as "Three D's— Dining, Drinking and Dancing—a place where you can bring your mother." The same article, however, quotes a sheepherder who commented, "I wouldn't want my mother to know I had ever been there."

Calamity Jane stayed at the brothel for some months, earning her keep by cooking and doing the laundry. That stint, however, proved to be her last job. While on a train to the little town of Terry in late July, drinking even more heavily than usual, Jane collapsed. She was taken to the Calloway Hotel in Terry and put in a small room.

Although treated by a doctor, she developed pneumonia and, according to some sources, inflammation of the bowels. Her health deteriorated quickly, and Martha Canary Burke—Calamity Jane— died on August 1, 1903. She was about 51 years old.

Calamity Jane's body was placed on public view in Terry so that mourners could pay their respects, but a wire cage had to be placed over the body's head to keep souvenir hunters from clipping locks of her hair. She was then taken to Deadwood and buried at Mount Moriah Cemetery, next to Wild Bill Hickok. The Society of Black Hills Pioneers paid for her funeral expenses.

According to legend, being buried next to Hickok was her last request. Four of the men who planned her funeral later stated that they had laid her to rest beside Hickok because, when the gambler was alive, he had had no use for her. They thought it would be a good joke on him.

Whichever story is true, Wild Bill's family was upset that the two had been buried side by side. Sol Star, the county clerk (and a Deadwood pioneer), wrote to the family in an effort to smooth over their feelings. Quoted in Joseph G. Rosa's book *Wild Bill Hickok*, Star noted: "[R]ecords show that a lot was purchased alongside and outside of the lot (fenced) of your Brother's for the burial of Calamity Jane, and said lot does in no wise [way] conflict or disturb the resting place of J.B."

Jane's funeral was the largest ever to be held in Deadwood for a woman. Allegedly, Calamity Jane's coffin was closed by a man whom she had nursed back to health when he was a young victim of the smallpox epidemic in Deadwood.

Calamity Jane was gone—but her death was far from being from the end of her legend.

7

CALAMITY JANE'S LEGACY

At first, it did not seem certain that Calamity Jane's memory would remain in the public consciousness. In the years immediately after her death, in fact, Jane slowly fell into obscurity.

During these years, there were only a few instances of Calamity Jane's name coming to public attention. One of them involved a cannon in World War I that was nicknamed Calamity Jane. According to legend, a group of soldiers who came from South Dakota used it to fire the last artillery shot of the conflict in 1918. There were also sporadic stories about her in newspapers, and a few books about her were published. This written material was generally filled with the incorrect or imaginary stories that had swirled around Jane for years.

Adding to the spread of inaccurate stories about Calamity Jane was the first film about her, which was made in the earliest days of the movie industry. This was a silent drama called *Wild Bill and Calamity Jane in the Days of '75 and '76*. The plot of this 1915 movie was almost completely invented; for example, in it Jane and Wild Bill get married, and he is murdered shortly afterward by Jack McCall, who is jealous of Hickok for winning Jane's hand.

During World War I, soldiers from South Dakota fired the last artillery shot of the war in Meuse, France, from the cannon that they named Calamity Jane.

Nonetheless, despite such occasional signs of recognition, Jane remained largely forgotten in the first decades of the twentieth century. She could easily have become nothing more than a minor footnote in the history of the Old West. McLaird's book notes: "For nearly two decades after Martha Canary's death . . . it seemed that she might be forgotten." However, the 1920s saw a change in this. People became curious once again about the frontierswoman's life and times. This newfound interest was part of a wave of nostalgia for the Old West that was sweeping America.

This national nostalgia arose, in large part, because of America's increasing industrialization and urbanization. Cities and towns were rapidly taking the place of rural areas, and millions of people were leaving the countryside in favor of better jobs in the nation's cities. As the frontier and the days of the untamed Wild West began disappearing, the relatively civilized residents of urban America became increasingly eager to hear about the old days of lawlessness and wide-open spaces.

One story from those old days, of course, was that of Calamity Jane. As a result, films and articles in magazines and newspapers about her began appearing with more regularity. For example, several more movie versions of Jane's life appeared. One of them repeated the familiar but false belief that she and Wild Bill had been romantically linked.

The movie's inaccuracies drew an angry response from none other than Wild Bill Hickok's nephew. Quoted in Rosa's book, Howard L. Hickok commented, "Imagine how our family felt, the uncle whose memory we loved and revered, portrayed on the nation's screen as the lover of Calamity Jane; married to a grand good woman, our aunt Agnes, [but] mixed up with Calamity (whose shortcomings had been known to us for years) a few short months later."

Despite such criticism, however, the public's interest in Jane's life continued to swell. By the end of the 1920s, thousands of visitors had come to Deadwood to pay their respects to the graves of the celebrated Wild Bill and Calamity Jane. Local residents were quick to take advantage of this influx of tourists. In 1929, an annual celebration honoring the two was organized in Deadwood.

Serious historians also began taking new looks at Jane and her wild reputation. Some of them recognized her as being a role model, pioneering the fight for women's equality—especially the right to tackle tough jobs normally reserved for men.

McLaird's book quotes one of these specialists in the history of the Old West, William E. Connelley. In 1933, Connelley went so far as to compare Calamity Jane to towering figures from history: Queen Elizabeth I of England and Empress Catherine of Russia. In his opinion, the frontierswoman resembled these rulers, who were

Buffalo Bill Remembers
His Old Friend

Buffalo Bill Cody made these remarks about Calamity Jane soon after her death. They were published in *The Livingston* (Montana) *Enterprise* on August 8, 1903, in an article titled "Calamity is Dead," and are reprinted on the Web site *cowgirls.com*. It gives a sense of Cody's admiration for his friend:

> I do not know much about her early life. . . . She had friends and very positive opinions of the things that a girl could enjoy, and she soon gained a local reputation for daring horsemanship and skill as a rifle shot. Before she was 20 General Crook appointed her a scout under me. From that time on her life was pretty lively all the time. She had unlimited nerve and entered into the work with enthusiasm, doing good service on a number of occasions.
>
> Though she did not do a man's share of the heavy work, she has gone in places where old frontiersmen were unwilling to trust themselves, and her courage and good-fellowship made her popular with every man in the command.

"great half-masculine, half-feminine queens, who thought and ruled with the brains of men."

As Jane's celebrity status grew, some of her friends and acquaintances were frankly puzzled by it. To them, she was a colorful character, but hardly one who stood out from the many colorful but unknown characters of the Old West. Typical of their comments was one quoted in McLaird's book, from a man who had served as one of Calamity's pallbearers. He wondered, "Now who in the world would think that Calamity Jane would get to be such a famous woman?"

Some of her contemporaries, meanwhile, tried to put Jane's increasing fame into sharper perspective. They argued that she was simply not worthy of serious historical consideration. For example, as quoted in "The Real Calamity Jane," an article by Margot Mifflin on the Web site Salon.com, two pioneers who wrote in 1924 about the Black Hills gold rush acknowledged that Jane had done admirable work in caring for the ill. Nevertheless, they also stated that Calamity Jane was "nothing more than a common [scarlet lady], drunken, disorderly and wholly devoid of any conception of morality."

THE MYSTERY OF CALAMITY JANE'S DAUGHTER

One of the enduring mysteries about Jane's life is the question of her daughter. Some historians doubt she ever existed, suggesting that the girl Calamity Jane called Jessie was not biologically hers. Others take it for granted that the girl was indeed Jane's, accepting one or another of the many conflicting stories that Jane and others told.

Assuming that Jessie really existed, and that Jane was her natural mother, there are still many unanswered questions about the girl. One of these concerns is simply what the child's name was. Some sources refer to her as Jane, although most call her Jessie.

A more important question has to do with the identity of Jessie's father. At various times in her life, Calamity stated that Jessie's father was Wild Bill Hickok. At others, she said it was the man she met in Texas, Clinton Burke. Some historians have speculated that the father was Bill Steers or one of the many other men who lived with Jane, or were at least involved with her.

Perhaps the most important question of all about Jessie has to do with her whereabouts in the years after Jane's death. What happened to her? Was she given up for adoption, as some people have claimed? Where was she raised?

Over the years, several women have claimed to be Calamity Jane's daughter. One of the most prominent of these surfaced in the 1930s: a Los Angeles resident named Jessie Oakes. During this time, Oakes wrote to various historical groups, newspapers, and government offices asking for information about Calamity Jane. Oakes said that family members had told her, all her life, that she was Jane's granddaughter.

The family connection between Calamity Jane and Jessie Oakes was never ultimately proved, although strong evidence suggests that it is correct. Some historians have speculated that Jessie Oakes was, in fact, Calamity Jane's daughter. They point to Oakes having memories of living with Jane that had sharp and plausible details that agreed with Jane's known whereabouts and activities.

Further speculation has suggested that Jessie was given up for adoption, but that her adoptive parents (on their own or with Jane's knowledge) led the girl to believe that the famous frontierswoman was her grandmother. McLaird, the author of the most definitive biography so far of the famous frontierswoman, believes that the Los Angeles woman was indeed Calamity Jane's natural child. He flatly states, "Jessie Oakes was undoubtedly Martha's daughter."

CLAIMING TO BE JESSIE

The other person who claimed to be Jane's offspring went public some years later. In 1941, a woman who said her name was Jean Hickok Burkhardt McCormick announced on a radio show that her parents were Martha Jane Canary and James Butler (Wild Bill) Hickok. According to her story, Jean McCormick had been born in 1873 in Montana. A sea captain named James O'Neil, who worked for the Cunard Line, was present and helped Jane recuperate from the birth.

He offered to take the infant and raise her with more opportunities than she would have on the frontier. Allegedly, Jane wanted to do what was best for her daughter, so she allowed O'Neil and his wife to take Jessie. The couple then raised the girl in England and Richmond, Virginia.

As evidence of the truth of her story, McCormick offered a diary, a deathbed statement, and a bundle of unsent letters that Jane had supposedly written to her. These were allegedly found among Jane's meager belongings after her death. McCormick also produced what she claimed was a marriage certificate, written in a Bible, showing that Martha Jane Canary and James Butler Hickok were wed at Benson's Landing, Montana Territory, in September 1875.

The alleged daughter's case was full of holes, and to most serious historians today it appears undeniable that her story was a complete invention. For one thing, McCormick's documents appear to be blatant forgeries—and not very good ones, at that.

One indication of this is that the letters and diary are written in an ornate and flowery style. Typical of the prose is this excerpt, reprinted in McLaird's book: "[T]he sunshine crept softly down between the tree branches seeming to spread a glory of radiant light about a group of friends gathered there ... like a benediction." This educated and erudite style is remarkable considering that the alleged author was, in all likelihood, illiterate.

Furthermore, in the many interviews she gave, McCormick provided information that was significantly inconsistent and conflicting. For example, her claims of the years she spent in Virginia and England do not fit other aspects of the time frame she outlined for herself. For another, the Cunard Line never employed a captain named O'Neil, and the photo McCormick supplied and said was of him was, in fact, a picture of a completely different person—a captain who really did sail for Cunard.

When these and other discrepancies were pointed out, McCormick became furious. She apparently formed a vehement dislike of the Hickok family for doubting her, accusing them of deliberately and falsely denying her claims. She also apparently grew increasingly desperate to prove the validity of her claims, continually providing "new" documents that, she said, had just come to light.

For the 10 years after her first announcement, until her death in 1951, McCormick insisted that she was the daughter of Calamity Jane and Wild Bill Hickok. Despite clear indications to the contrary, many people accepted her story as truth. These included writers who produced biographies of Calamity Jane during this time, as well as government officials. In fact, according to federal records, the U.S. Department of Public Welfare, late in McCormick's life, granted her an old-age assistance pension.

As a result of this acceptance, Jean McCormick's version of events entered the popular imagination and has remained there since. McLaird comments in his book, "McCormick's Calamity Jane is vastly different from the actual Martha Canary. Yet, despite McCormick's factual errors, misinformation, and personal vendettas, her documents have secured a permanent place in Calamity Jane folklore, an amazing feat for a clumsy forgery."

THE LEGEND LIVES ON

What McLaird aptly calls "Calamity Jane folklore"—that is, the trove of highly imaginative or completely invented stories about her life—is still repeated and augmented today. A number of sources have contributed to this. One such source of dubious biographical information is Hollywood.

A number of films about Calamity Jane have come from there in the years since the early silent era. In 1936, for example, the legendary Cecil B. DeMille directed *The Plainsman*. This movie tells a highly fictionalized account of the relationships between Wild Bill Hickok (played by Gary Cooper), Calamity Jane (played by Jean Arthur), Buffalo Bill Cody, and George Custer. The film's scrambled timeline and story go so far as to include a scene in which Abraham Lincoln sets the stage for Hickok's adventures, despite the fact that Hickok was an obscure mule-team driver when Lincoln was in office.

Later films or made-for-TV movies about her have been equally fanciful. They have starred actresses as different from one another as Jane Russell, Doris Day (in a musical version of Calamity Jane's life), Anjelica Huston, Carol Burnett, and Ellen Barkin. A more nuanced and believable portrayal of Jane appeared in the gritty TV series *Deadwood*, in which she was a major character. A gifted actress, Robin Weigert, played Jane as deeply flawed and foulmouthed, but also sympathetic and likeable.

A number of novels have also used Calamity Jane's story. One of these is Pete Dexter's *Deadwood*, which formed the basis for the television series. Another is Larry McMurtry's *Buffalo Girls*.

For many years after Calamity Jane's death, it seemed as if she would be forgotten. By the 1920s, however, people began to look back to the frontier period with nostalgia. Colorful characters like Wild Bill Hickok, Wyatt Earp, and Calamity Jane (portrayed here by actress Robin Weigert in the TV series *Deadwood*) have remained popular ever since, despite claims of exaggeration and embellishment.

A prominent Texas novelist who sets many of his books in the Old West, McMurtry used his book to speculate on one theory about Jane that has been suggested in the past: that she was a hermaphrodite.

"CALAMITY JEANS" AND MORE

In addition to books, movies, and television, there are many more modern references to Calamity Jane. A number of Web sites are devoted to her, or at least contain extensive amounts of information about her. She continues to be the subject of numerous articles in newspapers and magazines.

Jane has been featured as well in dozens of other venues, including animated cartoons, comic books, plays, a musical, slot machines, video games, dolls, postcards, T-shirts, and more. Both a golf putter and a golf tournament have been named in her honor, as well as a line of jeans called (naturally) "Calamity Jeans."

Several restaurants, gift shops, and other businesses are also named after Calamity Jane. In the town of Belle Fourche, South Dakota, where Calamity Jane spent her last months, a hair shop is named after her. (On the other hand, the town's Web site does not mention its famous guest's time there.) At least one Calamity Jane impersonator, an actress named Dianne Gleason, is available for hire at various functions, delivering a monologue about the frontierswoman's wild adventures.

Meanwhile, a number of monuments and museums, mostly in her beloved West, keep Jane's name alive. For example, in Rawlins, Wyoming, the Carbon County Museum has a small display dedicated to her time there. Also, Calamity Peak, a rock formation near what is now the town of Custer, South Dakota, is named after her.

For nearly a century, until it closed in 1990, Goldberg's Grocery Store in Deadwood maintained an invoice on its books for $7 in credit that Calamity Jane ran up in October 1895. In addition, Jane's hometown of Princeton, Missouri, has several memorials to her, including its annual Calamity Jane Days.

Given all this, and the public's continuing fascination with the figures of the Old West, there seems little chance of the famously rowdy Martha Jane Canary's legend disappearing anytime soon. As McLaird comments in his book, "It is doubtful Calamity's role in the folklore of the American West will ever diminish. Instead, the Calamity Jane legend will be remolded to meet the needs of each generation." After all, no matter how true the stories are, they are still good stories—and so Calamity Jane will continue to live on.

CHRONOLOGY

c. 1852   Martha is born to Robert and Charlotte Canary near Princeton, Missouri.

1862–1863   The Canary family moves to Montana Territory.

1866   Martha's mother dies.

TIMELINE

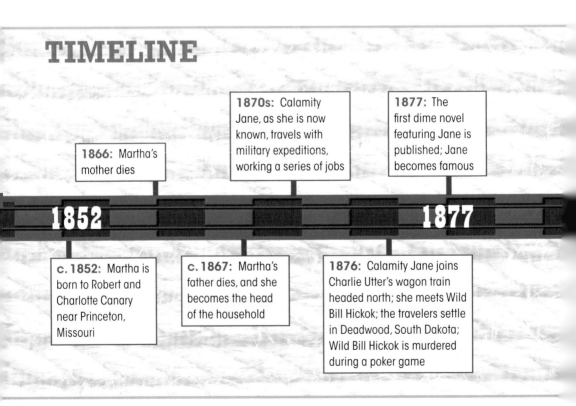

1866: Martha's mother dies

1870s: Calamity Jane, as she is now known, travels with military expeditions, working a series of jobs

1877: The first dime novel featuring Jane is published; Jane becomes famous

1852

1877

c. 1852: Martha is born to Robert and Charlotte Canary near Princeton, Missouri

c. 1867: Martha's father dies, and she becomes the head of the household

1876: Calamity Jane joins Charlie Utter's wagon train headed north; she meets Wild Bill Hickok; the travelers settle in Deadwood, South Dakota; Wild Bill Hickok is murdered during a poker game

c. 1867   Martha's father dies, and Martha becomes the head of the household of six children.

1868   Martha packs up her siblings and moves to Fort Bridger, Wyoming Territory. They move on to Piedmont, Wyoming.

1870s   Calamity Jane, as she is now known, travels with military expeditions. She works a series of jobs including dishwasher, cook, waitress, dance hall girl, nurse, oxen driver, and scout.

1876   While in Fort Laramie, Wyoming, Calamity Jane joins Charlie Utter's wagon train headed north. On that journey she meets Wild Bill Hickok. The

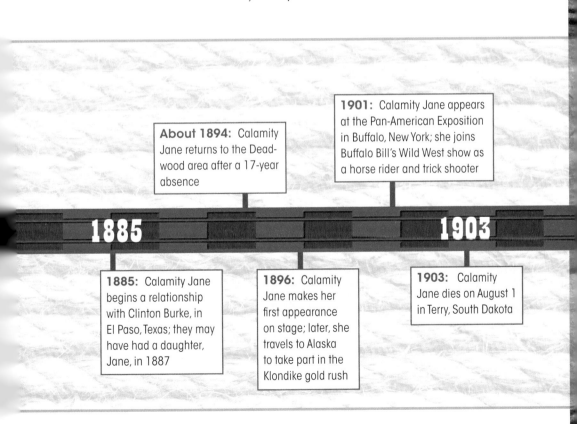

About 1894: Calamity Jane returns to the Deadwood area after a 17-year absence

1901: Calamity Jane appears at the Pan-American Exposition in Buffalo, New York; she joins Buffalo Bill's Wild West show as a horse rider and trick shooter

1885

1903

1885: Calamity Jane begins a relationship with Clinton Burke, in El Paso, Texas; they may have had a daughter, Jane, in 1887

1896: Calamity Jane makes her first appearance on stage; later, she travels to Alaska to take part in the Klondike gold rush

1903: Calamity Jane dies on August 1 in Terry, South Dakota

travelers settle in the Black Hills of Deadwood, Dakota Territory.

Wild Bill Hickok is murdered during a poker game that August. Calamity Jane claims to have married Hickok and had his child, although they barely knew each other.

1877   The first dime novel featuring Calamity Jane is published. Jane becomes famous.

Calamity Jane leaves Deadwood to wander the West.

1884   Calamity Jane moves to the gold boomtown of Eagle City, Idaho.

1885   After more traveling, Calamity Jane begins a relationship with Clinton Burke, in El Paso, Texas. Burke may have been the father of her daughter, Jane, who was possibly born in 1887. They move to Boulder, Colorado, in 1889 and open a hotel.

About 1894   Calamity Jane and her family travel through Wyoming, Montana, Idaho, Washington, Oregon, back to Montana, then to Dakota, returning to the Deadwood area after a 17-year absence.

1896   Calamity Jane makes her first appearance on stage at the Palace Museum in Minneapolis under the management of Kohl and Middleton. Later, she travels to Alaska to take part in the Klondike gold rush.

1901   Calamity Jane appears at the Pan-American Exposition in Buffalo, New York.

Calamity Jane joins Buffalo Bill's Wild West show as a horse rider and trick shooter.

1903   Calamity Jane dies on August 1 in Terry, South Dakota.

GLOSSARY

Beau Brummells   Fashion-conscious men.

boomtown   A rough town that develops quickly around a gold strike or other phenomenon.

broncho   A variant of "bronco," a wild horse.

buckskin   Animal hide used for clothing.

bullwhacker   The driver of a team of oxen.

cattle town   A destination for a cattle drive.

chestnut   An old term for a tired joke.

common-law marriage   When two people live together without marrying.

cream of tartar   A type of salt used in cooking.

derogatory   Insulting.

entrepreneur   Someone who starts his or her own small business.

Epsom salts   A chemical used medicinally.

equestrian   Having to do with horses.

faro   A popular card game of the Old West.

fording   Crossing a river.

hermaphrodite   A person born with the physical characteristics of both sexes.

husbandmen   Farmers.

livery   A place for the feeding, stabling, and caring of horses.

livestock   Animals on farms, especially cows.

matron   A female guard in a prison.

penny-a-liner   A hack writer.

pneumonia   A serious respiratory disease.

putter   A type of golf club.

quicksand   An unstable patch of wet ground that can suck people or animals down.

smallpox   A contagious and frequently fatal disease, characterized by fever, aches, and infected skin.

spittoon   A metal bowl in which tobacco chewers spit.

teamster   In the Old West, someone in charge of a freight coach drawn by a team of horses.

BIBLIOGRAPHY

Bankson, Russell A. *The Klondike Nugget* (Caldwell, Idaho). Available online. URL: http://www.arcticwebsite.com/Calamity-Jane.html.

"Calamity Jane." *Cowgirls.com*. Available online. URL: http://www.cowgirls.com/dream/cowgals/calamity.htm.

"Calamity Jane—Rowdy Woman of the West." *Legends of America*. Available online. URL: http://www.legendsofamerica.com/WE-CalamityJane2.html.

"Calamity Jane." *Pan-American Women*. Available online. URL: http://panam1901.bfn.org/documents/panamwomen/calamityjane.htm.

"The Custer Expedition," *Deadwood* magazine, July/August 1996. Available online. URL: http://www.deadwoodmagazine.com/archivedsite/Archives/CustExp.htm.

Franz, Mary. "The Real Men of Deadwood." *Wild West,* August 2006. Available online. URL: http://www.historynet.com/the-real-men-of-deadwood.htm.

"Girls of the Gulch." *Deadwood* magazine. Available online. URL: http://www.deadwoodmagazine.com/archivedsite/Archives/Girls_Belle.htm.

Lavery, David. *Reading Deadwood: A Western to Swear By.* New York: I.B. Tauris, 2006.

"Martha Jane 'Calamity Jane' Cannary." *Women in History*. Available online. URL: http://www.lkwdpl.org/wihohio/cana-mar.htm.

McLaird, James D. *Calamity Jane: The Woman and the Legend.* Norman, Okla.: University of Oklahoma Press, 2005.

Mifflin, Margot. "The Real Calamity Jane," *Salon*, December 6, 2005. Available online. URL: http://www.salon.com/books/review/2005/12/06/mclaird/index.html.

Moulton, Candy. "Following Calamity Jane," *True West*, January 6, 2010. Available online. URL: http://www.truewestmagazine.com/stories/following_calamity_jane/1370/3/.

Roberts, Phil. "Agnes Thatcher Lake: Equestrian Rider, Circus Performer, and Wild Bill's Wife." *University of Wyoming Academic Web*. Available online. URL: http://uwacadweb.uwyo.edu/RobertsHistory/buffalo_bones_wild_bill_marriage.htm.

Rosa, Joseph C. *Wild Bill Hickok: The Man and the Myth*. Lawrence, Kans.: University Press of Kansas, 1996.

Sollid, Roberta Beed. *Calamity Jane: A Study in Historical Criticism*. Helena, Mont.: Historical Society Press, 1995.

Weiser, Kathy. "Calamity Jane—Rowdy Woman of the West." *Legends of America*. January 2010. Available online. URL: http://www.legendsofamerica.com/WE-CalamityJane2.html.

"Wild Bill Cashed in his Last Chip in Deadwood." *Deadwood* magazine. Available online. URL: http://www.deadwoodmagazine.com/archivedsite/Archives/wildbill.htm.

FURTHER RESOURCES

Commire, Anne, editor. *Women in World History: A Biographical Encyclopedia*. Waterford, Conn.: Yorkin Publications, 1999–2000.

DuFran, Dora. *Low Down on Calamity Jane*. Stickney, S. Dak.: Argus Printers, 1981.

Faber, Doris. *Calamity Jane: Her Life and Her Legend*. Boston: Houghton Mifflin, 1992.

Krohn, Katherine E. *Women of the Wild West*. Minneapolis: Lerner Publications Co., 2000.

Mueller, Ellen Crago. *Calamity Jane*. Laramie, Wyo.: Jelm Mountain Press, 1981.

Riley, Glenda, editor. *By Grit & Grace: Eleven Women Who Shaped the American West*. Golden, Colo.: Fulcrum Publishing, 1997.

———.*Wild Women of the Old West*. Golden, Colo.: Fulcrum Publishing, 2003.

Sanford, William R., and Carl R. Green. *Calamity Jane: Frontier Original*. Springfield, N.J.: Enslow Publishers, 1996.

Films/DVD

Biography: Calamity Jane, DVD. New York: A&E Television Networks, 2008.

Calamity Jane, DVD. Directed by David Butler. 1953, Calabasas: Warner Bros. Pictures, 2005.

Deadwood: The Complete Series, DVD. Los Angeles: HBO, 2008.

Web Sites

The Adams Deadwood: Legendary and Historic Figures—Calamity Jane

http://www.adamsmuseumandhouse.org/adamscharacters_detail.php?id=6

This site, maintained by the Adams Museum & House, the oldest history museum in Deadwood, South Dakota, has a short biography of Calamity Jane.

Cowgal's Home on the Web: Calamity Jane

http://www.cowgirls.com/dream/cowgals/calamity.htm

This site about Calamity Jane has some interesting quotes from Buffalo Bill Cody.

Life and Adventures of Calamity Jane by Herself

http://pinkmonkey.com/dl/library1/digi457.pdf

This site reproduces Calamity's short autobiography in its entirety.

Women of the American West

http://www.legendsofamerica.com/WE-Women.html

This site has biographical information and photographs of the women who settled the frontier, including Calamity Jane, Belle Starr, and Kitty Leroy.

PICTURE CREDITS

Page

INDEX

ABOUT THE AUTHOR

Adam Woog has written many books for adults, young adults, and children. He has a special interest in biography and history. Woog lives with his wife in his hometown of Seattle, Washington. They have a college-age daughter.